This excellent
work answers serious
questions we all
have about faith.

I've met the
author personally.

your friend

appleseed
press
www.appleseedpress.org

Jesus:
the only way?

■ john snyder

babylon, new york, u.s.a.

© 2005 by John Snyder
First Printing, 2006
Second Printing, 2007

Published by Appleseed Press
Babylon, New York, U.S.A.

Printed in the U.S.A.

ISBN-10: 0-9764256-0-2
ISBN-13: 978-0976425601

Library of Congress Control Number: 2005906028

Cover design by Nous Trois
Interior design by Sarah Snyder & Stephanie Snyder

contents

Summary and Conclusion

Appendix A
The Claims

Appendix B
The Repentance of Rudolf Bultmann

Appendix C
The Bishop's Move: The Case of John A. T. Robinson

Notes

Bibliography

Index

preface

We enjoy a good Hollywood adventure film while knowing full well that we are viewing a complete fantasy. The skill of the director is tested by how believable he or she can make the story, but we still know that the world pictured before us is not the real world. Nevertheless, when the movie is over and we imagine ourselves to be reentering the realm of real things, it's entirely possible for us to walk out of a dark theater into bright sunlight outside and enter a fantasy far more profound than anything we have just viewed on the big screen.

Think about the magnitude of this dream world. If we were to believe with all sincerity in a God who didn't really exist, who would doubt that life lived with such a false belief would be a life of fantasy? On the other hand, it would be just as much a fantasy not to believe in a God who really was there. To go about our daily business believing with all our heart anything which is untrue about life's origin, meaning, or destiny, or somehow failing to believe what is true, would be to exist in a dark room of fiction and illusion.

In the pages that follow, we'll consider these questions: When it comes to religion, do we turn from the logic, reason, and plain common sense we apply to everything else in life and allow ourselves to enter a shadow world of delusion far exceeding that of the sci-fi or spy thriller? Do we easily accept notions from others that we would not tolerate for a moment in any other area of life? Do we grant free passes to ways of thinking that we would instantly reject if they came to us under any other name than that of religion? Do we find ideas hard to believe or even personally offensive because they seem untrue, or because they are unwelcome?

Whereas Hollywood is able to take fiction and make it appear real, our world can take the real and make it appear a mere tale. It is for sorting out truth from fiction that this book is written.

acknowledgments

A book usually has only one author but is the final product of many hands and minds. Like the seemingly endless credits at the end of a film, so is the list of those who in one way or another contribute to a book's existence. Unlike a film, not everyone, or even most, can be mentioned. There are simply too many to cite, but some who mustn't be overlooked.

Always first in my life of those who make books possible is my family. Each is a brilliant writer and proofreader in her own right and each has special gifts in editing and suggestion making. I depend heavily upon them in the gathering, organizing, and presentation of the material. They work as hard as I do in the labor of it all.

In addition, I could not fail to thank those who have assisted us along the way with critical remarks. I am particularly indebted to Andrew Craig, Steve Marmaroff, Greg Nulty, Ruth Trevithick, and Dietrich Wichmann for their talents in spotting things which I could not see and in providing valuable counsel along the way.

Many thanks to Sarah Snyder and Stephanie Snyder for the cover and interior design.

For any basic weaknesses and omissions of the work I alone must be held responsible.

introduction

A young Chinese student related his ordeal of how he crossed the Yalu River one terrifying night, seeking to escape the oppressions of his Communist government in hopes of finding freedom somewhere in the world. He was aware that in those hours in the dark water, hanging between life and death, there was someone else there. Who it was, he couldn't tell, but he was absolutely sure that there was someone assisting him – some invisible, intelligent being. He hoped that by studying with us he could find the answer to what all this meant for him.

A very quiet man told of how, just a year earlier, he was lying in a hospital bed in Philadelphia, knowing only that he was dying and there was nothing anyone could do for him. One night his whole room suddenly filled up with a radiant light. It remained for less than a minute. There was no voice, no explanation, no message, nothing. But the next day he began to feel differently. Days later, he checked out of the hospital. Shortly afterwards, he joined us just to find out what happened that night and who or what it was that entered his room and gave back his life.

I related that on the day of my birth I was inadvertently switched in the hospital in Glendale, California, and given to the wrong family. Only by the most amazing series of coincidences was I restored to my rightful parents. Years later, my life was saved on a lonely mountain road by a voice warning of danger ahead. Several other events during the course of my youth convinced me that someone out there had an interest in my existence and apparently wanted something from me. I was now engaged in a long-term pursuit of the One who had brushed so closely to me.

There were plenty of those among us who had no extraordinary events occur in their lives. They were there just in search of some meaning or purpose in life, thinking that such things may have some connection to the events which took place nearly two millennia earlier.

Whatever our particular reasons, we were all there: ex-gang leaders, witches, marxist revolutionaries (this was the late 1960s), priests and nuns, attorneys, psychologists, philosophers, draft dodgers, and a whole zoo of other characters who had their own accounts to give.

All of us had enrolled in theological seminary, many believing that our answers might be found in the man Jesus. But why did so many very diverse people from so many vastly different backgrounds conclude that their answers could be found in him rather than in some other person or philosophy? What is there about Jesus of Nazareth that so profoundly overshadows all other historical characters and attracts to himself such a wide variety of personalities? There's no other person in history who creates for us so many puzzling questions and yet seems to hold in his hand all the final answers.

I've tried to condense a great deal of research into a fairly brief presentation to explain why Jesus holds such a fascination for at least one-third of the earth's population. Also, I wanted to account for why, when people are given the intellectual freedom to search on their own, they instinctively check into the Jesus question. Why do people from every conceivable walk of life and from every religion and philosophy testify that in him they've found the answers to life's greatest riddles?

But even more than that, why are there so many things claimed about Jesus that are claimed by or about no one else in history? How can it be insisted that life's most decisive answers just can't be found elsewhere? One reason may be that of all those of the past who might be selected as a reference point and guide for human life, Jesus is the only one who said that he would be accessible to the human race in every generation. He is the only one in history who said he would (or even could) be there for us, whether among the perils of the Yalu River, the hospital room, or the winding mountain road.

This book is a short version of a very long and detailed story, but in these pages it should become crystal clear why all these extravagant statements about Jesus are made and whether or not any truly thinking person can embrace them with their entire heart and mind.

1:
the human factor

The Hard Questions

"Surely you don't believe that there is only one way to God and salvation, do you?!"

"Do you mean to tell me that every Jew, every Hindu, every Muslim, Shinto, and Buddhist is wrong, but that you, the Christian, are right?! Aren't you trying to play the role of God?"

"Isn't all this ancient business about Jesus far too narrow for our modern inclusive age?"

In our day, this exclusivity is undoubtedly our number one objection to Christian faith, or any faith that sees itself as the one and only way. Initially, it seems easy to understand why this is so. It's considered completely outdated to suggest that Jesus Christ, or any other figure, is the only way to God and the sole means of eternal salvation. The claim is deemed the height of narrowness, ethnocentrism, and just plain bigotry, so offensive to the intellect as to warrant instant and unqualified censure. The idea is not even seriously entertained in enlightened circles.

How many devout, well-intentioned believers have been stopped cold in their tracks by the paralyzing questions mentioned above? The questions are typically posed with utmost confidence and there's-not-much-left-to-talk-about finality. The only possible answer appears to be, "Well, since you put it that way, it does pose a problem, doesn't it?" Or, "No, I didn't mean exactly *that*." Or perhaps even more often, "Uh, well, er...I guess that's what I mean."

If this most extraordinary statement about Jesus being the only way to God really is true, then the believer can answer the honest questioner with something like this: "Yes, of course I do. Don't you?! I'd like to offer some easily discoverable facts that would make it difficult to arrive at any other conclusion."

If such a candid response isn't possible, then the assertion will be regarded as merely a private religious conviction which isn't capable of being defended in the public marketplace. If these discoverable facts exist, then they should be capable of presentation without a great deal of humming and hawing.

Putting Things in Perspective

One of the chief reasons why this claim to the uniqueness of Christ is considered so totally unbelievable today (even cruel or heartless) is that it is usually viewed in isolation from the total picture. But what if it's placed in a different setting?

Take, for example, the person who says, "I can't believe in some invisible God or in any of those other invisible beings and places that religious people are always telling me about. If I can't see, hear, touch, or smell something, I'm not interested!" This may not be everyone's objection, but you've probably heard it or something similar.

Let's try viewing this sort of thinking in light of what we can come to know without much effort. See this from the point of view of basic physics or chemistry. Try to remember from your lessons what you answered when your instructor asked the question, "What are four of the physical forces?" If you answered, "Electromagnetic, gravitational, centrifugal, and centripetal forces," or some such thing, you passed the test. If you answered, "Don't give me any of that stuff about the forces, because I can't see, hear, touch, or smell them!" you would have flunked your course and probably been invited to change your major! What all these forces have in common is that each is invisible.

Things get even stickier as you go up the scientific ladder. Not only are the fundamental forces incapable of being seen, heard, touched, or smelled, but the physical world does not always lend itself to such simple measurements. Matter, the stuff we are able to discern with our eyes and touch with our fingers, is only an infinitesimally small part of what is right in front of us all the time.

Thus a great deal of what is "real" about our world is not perceivable by our senses. All kinds of yet undiscovered things could exist at the same time in the same space as that which we see. We reach this conclusion only by acquiring more facts.

The situations of previous generations were similar. At one time, most thinking people were sure that the world was flat or that the earth was the center of the universe. Such beliefs were just too obvious for people even to argue. Many of the greatest intellects of their time were absolutely convinced that these cherished ideas were beyond dispute, while a few other great thinkers were denied high career positions because they thought otherwise. The vast majority believed that those who disagreed on these most "basic truths" were unstable in mind and ought to be carefully watched! It was only more information about the universe that eventually rendered the prevailing opinions obsolete.

It is common to our experience of life: What seems to make sense to our limited understanding disappears like a morning haze as the sunlight of knowledge dawns. Just as a dream that makes so much sense while sleeping becomes pure foolishness in the light of morning, so many of our deepest convictions about life fade from view when confronted with more and more plain fact.

Is it possible that we can begin to understand the puzzling claim that Jesus is the only way to God and the only hope of salvation in the light of more information? Are facts from history and the sciences friends or enemies of such faith? Can it be that what appears to us as the height of ignorance, ethnocentrism, and even heartless intolerance at the beginning of our search might come to seem as just everyday common sense when we fill in the picture with more factual details?

Let's begin just as we did with the assumption about the physical world around us, that we might need more information before making a decision one way or the other. We'll at least leave the question wide open.

It's an old-fashioned idea but still true: Reality is reality, with or without our consent. Science teaches us that the more we come to understand our universe, the more we should be slow to believe or disbelieve something based upon our limited understanding or perception of what is. We need more knowledge before making critical life decisions.

Can we work our way through the forest of popular fiction about Jesus to the open country of truth? Great numbers of honest, skeptical, thinking people through the ages have taken this journey before us. Where do the facts lead?

Some Roadblocks Ahead

A few warning signs appear at the beginning of our journey. One thing we all know about ourselves, just from our own personal experience of life, is that in many ways we can be tricked and misled. We are often easy prey to illusions, mirages, and seductive sales pitches. We are prone to self-delusion of all kinds. Sometimes we find ourselves falling for just about any idea under the sun simply because we would rather believe in comfortable fiction than in painful truth.

Regardless of our differences, life teaches each of us that the most appealing belief for the moment may be in the long run the least beneficial to us. What looks good initially may not have any substance to it at all. Moreover, truth (if there is any to be found) is difficult to locate and nail down no matter what topic we are considering, whether questions about life and death or even about what happened on the street corner just twenty minutes ago. Typically, it doesn't lie on the surface of things and most often requires a bit of exploring.

Postmodern Thinking

What has been mentioned briefly about the variety of ways we fool ourselves can be observed more closely in what has now become known as postmodern thinking. We hear the words more and more often in the news and in popular literature. Exactly what is it?

Postmodern thinking operates on the assumption that there are no absolute ways of viewing reality – it's all merely a personal and relative matter. You may have your own standards of what is real, true, right, or wrong, and I may have mine. You can't impose your truth on me and I can't impose mine on you. We might even hold two or three mutually contradictory ideas at the same time and it really doesn't seem to pose a problem. A unified, coherent view of all truth is not possible or even desirable.

When it comes to questions about God, Jesus, absolute truth, ethics, morals, and all the rest, something very interesting happens. We resist vigorously by means of postmodern thought the very thing we demand in every other department of life. We may choose to deny the possibility of absolutely clear and unambiguous statements about God or defy those offered to us. Yet when it comes to every other facet of reality, we not only welcome clear and straightforward statements of what is, but scoff when it's suggested that everything might be relative or that all ideas are of equal value.

In physics, for example, we accept the notion that things are the way they are and there isn't much we can do about it. Gravity is gravity, and although some may choose not to believe in it themselves, we agree that they will do well to follow the example of those who do. The patterns or "laws" of physics are not just imagination, and to deny them is to put ourselves in a certain amount of danger. When the professor is telling us about them we are expected to write them down, learn them, and believe them with all our heart. He doesn't go around the classroom and inquire how we personally feel about them or ask for our individual slant on the matter.

It's the same in the fields of chemistry, aerodynamics, math, and all the rest. We expect to hear that certain facts stand by themselves apart from our feelings and attitudes toward them. We expect statements about there being a correct way and an incorrect way to see things just because that's the way they are. We don't have to like them; we just need to accept them. We want (we demand!) that our pilots, our bridge engineers, auto mechanics, surgeons, dentists, and pharmacists believe that there is a clear, absolutely right way and a wrong way of doing things. To believe anything else would spell great disaster.

Think for a moment how this kind of postmodern thinking would work out in real life. The philosophy professor who sells his students the notions of postmodernism could not possibly live consistently with the results of his teaching. Someone who writes books arguing that there could be no absolute truths, values, or morals in life would be very angry if he lost his retirement investments accumulated from book royalties because the CEO of a company in which he was heavily invested lived out the relativist values which he espoused to his students.

The professor would also expect that, at least in practice, the publisher of his books on moral relativism, the postal workers who delivered them, the managers of the bookstores who sold them, his bankers who kept his money safe, and so forth would not follow the teaching of postmodernism. Otherwise, he could not even sustain his activities of teaching others and writing that there are no absolute truths or moral values. His very lifeblood comes from the "old ways" of thinking. The successful and prosperous professor of intellectual, moral, and ethical relativism enjoys living off the fat of the land created and sustained by the very things he speaks against.

In earlier days of logic and reason, whenever the claims of some belief system were made, the response from the skeptic was in the form of evidence, logic, and rational argument. The objector would attempt to produce facts from any reliable source to demonstrate that such a view was either untrue or unreasonable. The defender of the belief would do the same thing. Evidence was gathered and presented from every corner to prove that the conviction was true and reasonable. Both were operating by the same rules.

Today, illogical and inconsistent thinking is not only considered seriously, it's often regarded with great honor.

Teachers and students alike can sustain mutually contradictory ideas on virtually all topics and feel quite at ease about it. It doesn't usually work too well in the chemistry lab (things tend to explode), but it's thought to work well in most of the social sciences.

However, the follower of postmodern thinking will inevitably run up against the brick wall of reality when trying to apply it. It's easy to espouse the concepts in the lecture hall (in fact, such ideas could not have arisen except in a safe and comfortable environment), but when called upon to provide some concrete help in the rough and tumble of real life, they vanish like smoke in the wind.

The claim is probably true that in practice no one actually is, or can be, a consistent postmodern thinker. When it comes down to it, all of us are "old-fashioned" absolutists at one point or another. We just need to find exactly where that point is. We become absolutist when something hurts us, touches our loved ones, or affects our social standing or financial holdings. The man who argues for the legitimacy of pornography, for example, may protest strongly if the subject matter happens to be his own daughter!

To sum up, once we crack open the word "postmodernism" we discover that there's really nothing inside it. If the postmodernist claims, "There are no absolutes!" the most sensible response is, "Does that include the absolute statement you just made?" If it's asserted, "There is no real knowledge, no absolute reality, no absolute meaning to any claim, word, or belief," then we may ask, "Do you mean that there is no meaning to the claim you just made?" or, "Is there any reality behind the words you just used or the belief you just professed?"

We could create a long list of such internal contradictions with postmodernism. Here is just a short list:

- If, according to some, there is no real knowledge to be gained, then how does one *know* that there is no knowledge to be gained?

- Why deliver lectures and write books trying to convey that words have no meaning?

- Why produce random and meaningless art, music, and literature to convince us that art, music, and literature are meaningless?

- If logic and reason are mere illusions stemming from chance chemical reactions in the brain, then why try to argue the case with logic and reason?

- If absolute values don't exist, then on what grounds do we point out that racism, sexism, or hate speech are bad, that the holocaust was evil, or that any policy or movement deserves approval or condemnation?

How can we have it both ways? Either there is real meaning behind words, values, and beliefs, or there isn't. If there isn't, then the most honest response is silence. For the moment we open our mouths and say anything coherent at all, we are affirming that there is real knowledge, meaning, and value. Postmodernism becomes the Frankenstein monster that turns to destroy its own creators.

These matters will become clearer in a later chapter when we try to apply postmodern beliefs to the very practical issues relating to the world's highly diverse religions.

Leftover Naturalism

Another roadblock to clear, objective thinking about God-related issues is "naturalism," that leftover of the last few generations of philosophy. This is the notion that "nature" (what we can see, hear, touch, and measure scientifically) is all there is. There is nature, and nothing but nature. In philosophy class, it was called "nothing-but-ness." Nothing comes to us from outside the system – no God, no angels, no demons, no miracles, and so forth. This philosophy is the direct product of atheism, and when it is encountered in the physical sciences it is really nothing more than atheism dressed up as science.

Parenthetically, it could be said that to be a *consistent* naturalist would be to admit that since there is nothing outside the physical world (matter), then all our thoughts must be nothing but the products of random chemical reactions within the brain. Thus, they can't correspond to any reality outside the system. If so, they aren't to be trusted as guides to what is real or true. This means that the statement, "The philosophy of naturalism is true," is no more valuable or useful than the statement, "The philosophy of naturalism is false." All thoughts about philosophy (any philosophy) would have to be regarded as just random chemical reactions and nothing more.

But the naturalistic professor of philosophy usually doesn't tell us all this. Normally, he teaches his students that his ideas are true, worthy of being written down, committed to memory, and fed back to him with precision on exam day. If his students happen to be committed postmodernists (consistent naturalists), they will go one step beyond their professor and argue that since there is no difference between illusion and reality, one person's view of what is "real" is equal to that of another. They will say (rightly), "Our random chemical reactions are just as good as yours. It's all a matter of personal choice." But even this final assertion will have no real meaning. It's just another one of those pesky chemical reactions!

We are faced here with the same kind of dilemma which confronted Charles Darwin who, near the end of his life, realized that if he was right in concluding that we are the descendants of monkeys, then how can we trust the convictions of a monkey's mind? In a similar way, if our thoughts are merely random chemical reactions in the brain, then how reliable are they?[1]

But back to the main track. To climb the ladder of success as a scientist today is more or less to give assent to the philosophy of naturalism, or at least to remain uncritical of it publicly. Of course, this wasn't true with the first scientists of the modern era, most of whom were committed believers in God. Modern science as we know it followed on the heels of the Reformation (when there was a deliberate return to biblical views and values) and in many ways was a direct product of it. But over time naturalism was promoted to the high rank it enjoys today. Gradually, the laws in nature came to be viewed independently from the Law-Giver. The connection between the two was forgotten.

The practical result of this is that the scientist will often tend to begin with the assumptions of naturalism when investigating the world. When we begin with naturalism, however, we end up with naturalism. What we *conceive* will determine what we *perceive*. There is an old Indian saying: The eye will not see what the mind does not want. The scientist who starts with the personal faith that all things can be explained by what we can observe with our naturalistic eyes will draw conclusions that will be in line with that faith. But there's really nothing in the entire realm of science that forces us to believe in this creed.

It's simply the social and political pressure to be like those around us and the desire to be respected by our peers that forces so many scientists into this mold. To step out of line with the herd and make statements (or even raise questions) that sound like God may exist or that the universe may be the product of design can quickly jeopardize our standing with our superiors. Entire careers hang in the balance.

For us, this means that if someone has been trained to think naturalistically, then they will tend to rule out the possibility that God can come to us from outside the system and declare Himself to us in a clear way. The only way out of the bottle is to exit the way we came in. Only by returning to a position of at least neutrality or openness can we begin where we need to begin. We must return to the place of the first scientific explorers who thought that scientific discovery was merely to follow wherever the facts may lead without worrying about whom it may offend or alienate.

The Three Minds

Another major roadblock to arriving at the truth about anything is our own personal mindset. Today, there are three kinds of minds. The first is the closed mind. It's closed to any new ideas or to anything that causes it discomfort. It resists any view which challenges what it imagines it already knows. It can reside equally within the devoutly religious person or the secular scientist.

The second is the totally "open mind." It's open at both ends. It allows any and all thoughts to pass through it like water through a channel, but nothing really gets lodged permanently. What goes in eventually goes out. No fundamental ideas stay long enough to form a lasting foundation to build on or act as a filter of other ideas. Each one is thought to be as good as any other. What is right or true is entirely up to the individual and may vary with the direction of the wind.

The third kind of mind is open on one end and closed on the other. It allows ideas to enter freely but is quick to assess them by what has been allowed to stay as true. It contains and retains basic, foundational ideas as the measure of all others and tosses out those which can't stand up to them. Such a mind fills up with those new ideas which are in accord with the basics and allows to spill over the side those which are of no use in helping to construct what we used to know as the "educated mind."

The third kind is what is required to return to some sanity about what is real and what is unreal. The second kind is that which we see gaining more and more ground around us. It's now widely considered to be an advanced or "progressive" form of thinking.

In truth, it's not a form of progress at all. It looks suspiciously like a reenactment of the event recorded in the Old Testament book of Genesis (3:5), the attempt of the first humans to "know good and evil," namely, to claim determinative authority to decide for themselves what constitutes good and evil, right and wrong, truth and falsehood.[2] This way of thinking may be seen rightly as a regression to our earliest, most primitive history – the folly of attempting to create our own private reality.

Is there a way we can get ourselves out of this current state of messy thinking? The Gospel of Jesus declares unequivocally that he only is the way out, the center of all truth about God, the world, and human life, the key to all that has real meaning. This sweeping statement is either true or it's false. If false (or indefensible) it deserves to have no time wasted on it. If true, nothing else would matter more.

Since both the believer in Jesus and the skeptic have an account to give for what they hold to be true, we shall go one more step and cross-examine the logical alternative to the Christian view. If Jesus is not the only way, what are the problems to face then?

Considering the matters involved, we are automatically under a moral obligation to apply our highest level of intelligence and honesty to the search.

2:
getting the questions right

Obviously, the first question to be asked about the claims of Jesus is: What exactly are they? Most people, believers and unbelievers alike, are unable to give even a summary of what they are. To correct this, we need to understand precisely what kind of Jesus is portrayed in the New Testament. This might sound a bit too elementary, but as we shall see, unless we grasp the height and depth of what is actually asserted about Jesus of Nazareth, every other question we ask later will be pointless.

Who Is the Jesus of the New Testament?

Even if you've already studied the issue in detail, the next section will be very important to keep in the forefront of your mind. From the very first to the last pages of the New Testament, we encounter a person so unique and so extraordinary that the claims about him determine the limits within which we must evaluate them. The ancient texts speak for themselves, and from them a coherent picture emerges.

I've listed in this chapter the principal claims about Jesus to demonstrate this truth: Jesus' high status is not the product of just a few offhanded remarks here and there. Rather, the New Testament is thoroughly permeated with them. They lie not on the fringe, but at the very heart of the information about him.

Let's look now on our own at a sampling of the statements within each layer of tradition. Later, we may consult the theologians and philosophers. According to most scholars, the Apostle Paul is regarded as the earliest of the Jesus sources. We'll start with his writings:

Romans 5:1–2
Access to God is gained through Jesus Christ.

Romans 8:18–25
His work of rescue extends to the whole created physical order.

Romans 16:26
The Gospel of Jesus is for all nations.

2 Corinthians 5:19
In Christ, God was acting to reconcile the world to Himself.

Galatians 2:16
No human being will be saved by obedience to religious rites, rituals, or rules. Only trust in what Jesus did for us will lead us to God.

Ephesians 1:20–21
God raised Jesus from the dead and seated him at His

right hand in the heavenly realms, far above all rule and authority, power and dominion, and every title that can be given, not only in the present age but also in the one to come.

Ephesians 4:10
Jesus Christ ascended higher than all the heavens to fill the whole universe.

Philippians 2:6–7
Jesus Christ, being in very nature God, condescended to take upon himself the form of a servant, being made in human likeness.

Colossians 1:15–17
He is the expressed image of the invisible God, head over all creation. All things were created by him and for him. In him, all things in creation hold together.

2 Thessalonians 1:8–9
There will be eternal destruction for those who do not obey the Gospel of Jesus.

1 Timothy 2:3–6
There is only one God and only one mediator between God and man, Christ Jesus.

We now turn to a sampling of the evidence from the four Gospels:

Matthew 1:23
Jesus is called *Emmanuel*, God with us.

Matthew 10:32
Acknowledging or denying Jesus will be the basis for our being acknowledged or disowned before God.

Matthew 11:27
All things are committed to Jesus by God. No one knows the Son except the Father, and no one knows the Father except the Son and those to whom Jesus chooses to reveal Him.

Matthew 28:18–20
All authority in heaven and on earth has been given to him. He commands his followers to make disciples of all nations, baptizing them in the name of the Father, the Son, and the Holy Spirit, teaching them his commands. He will be with them until the end of the Age.

Mark 1:11
He is God's Son.

Mark 4:35–41
He controls the weather and natural phenomena.

Mark 6:45–52
He defies gravity.

Mark 9:36–37
Whoever welcomes Jesus welcomes God.

Mark 14:36
He calls God his "Daddy" or "Papa."

Luke 1:34–35
He is supernaturally born.

Luke 2:32
He is the light for the Gentiles and the source of salvation for all people.

Luke 2:49
As a boy, he was aware of an unparalleled relationship with God the Father.

Luke 3:17
The final judgment of humanity will occur with his return.

Luke 10:16
To reject him is to reject God.

Luke 10:22
No one comes to a knowledge of God unless Jesus grants permission.

Luke 24:5–7
His physical body is raised from death.

John 1:1
He is the Word who was with God in the beginning and who was God.

John 1:3
All that was made in creation was made through him.

John 1:14
The eternal Word, who was God, became human in Jesus. He is the only Son from the Father.

John 2:1–11
He manipulates and reorganizes molecules.

John 3:16
He is God's only Son. Whoever believes in him will not perish, but will have eternal life.

John 3:35
The Father loves the Son and has placed everything in his hands. Whoever rejects Jesus will not see life.

John 5:23
Whoever fails to honor the Son fails to honor the Father.

John 6:29
The principal work of God is for us to believe in Jesus, His Son.

John 6:46
No one has ever seen the Father except the Son.

John 10:30
He and the Father are one.

John 12:45
When we look at him, we see God.

John 14:6
He is the way, the truth, and the life. No one comes to the Father except through him.

John 17:5
He enjoyed glory with the Father even before the creation of the world.

John 20:28
> He was called "Lord" and "God."

In Luke's second book, traditionally called *The Acts of the Apostles*, he continues to record the work of the risen Jesus Christ in the life of the early church.

Acts 3:21
> He remains in heaven until his return to earth to restore all things.

Acts 4:12
> Human salvation is found in no other name on earth than Jesus Christ.

The remainder of the New Testament echoes many of the same themes as the letters of Paul, the Gospels, and Acts:

Hebrews 1:2
> He was appointed heir of all things, and through him God made the universe.

Hebrews 1:3
> He is the radiance of God's glory and the exact representation of His being, sustaining all things by his powerful word.

Hebrews 4:15
> He was without sin.

Hebrews 5:9
> He became the source of eternal salvation for all those who obey him.

1 Peter 3:22

He is now in heaven at God's right hand – with angels, authorities, and powers in submission to him.

1 John 2:23

No one who denies Jesus the Son has God the Father. He who confesses the Son has the Father also.

1 John 5:12

He who does not have the Son does not have life.

Revelation 1:5

He is the ruler of earthly kings.

Revelation 1:18

He holds the keys to death and Hades.

Revelation 22:13

He is the Alpha and Omega, the beginning and the end (the same title claimed by the Lord God in 1:8).

All the above is a representative but incomplete account of what the New Testament says about Jesus (see Appendix A for a more complete list). Keep in mind, at the moment we are simply listing what the claims are and reserving judgment as to whether we think they are true or false. We lay them before us in order to assess them. We are not reading them through the eyes of any theologian or philosopher.

One important lesson we may learn over many years of theological study is not to see the Bible through the lens of any one "expert" or rely upon the ever-shifting sands of scholarly opinion. Theories about Jesus or the Bible, like clothing fashions, come and go with predictable regularity. Even the one man known as the Grand Master of New

Testament skepticism, German professor Rudolf Bultmann, came to the end of life with a very high view of Scripture, preferring it to speak for itself without the aid of any human interpreter. Indeed, the evidence suggests that in his closing years he returned to the traditional faith of his youth (see Appendix B).

The New Testament has always been capable of standing on its own and speaking for itself without the aid of any particular human authority. Good scholarship (thankfully, there's plenty of it) allows the texts to speak for themselves by clarifying their original intent within their own contexts. It then tries to apply the results in a creative and intelligent way.

With all this in mind, let's draw the claims together and summarize them very briefly. This summary has been called "The Gospel," preached by missionaries and evangelists over the earth for the past 2,000 years. Its general outlines may be presented as follows:

> Jesus Christ is the unique Son of God who came into the world to reveal both who God is and what, by God's grace, a human being should be and one day will be. He calls people everywhere to be his disciples and follow him into the eternal kingdom of his Father. He paid the penalty for all our sins by his death on the cross and offers the free gift of forgiveness and eternal life to whomever comes to him in simple humility. His identity, authority, and ministry were validated and vindicated by his physical resurrection from the dead.
>
> Anyone who rejects him rejects the only true God and will be judged and eternally separated from God. All who gladly receive him will be received by God. In the end, they will be raised from death to life in transformed, physical bodies to live forever on a new, transformed earth where only truth, justice, and righteousness exist.

We can say a few things even before we begin to look at the overall picture with a more critical eye. We see immediately that we are not talking about just another person. He is portrayed as someone who has no equal in history and is so vastly different from the rest of humanity that we can't categorize him on the same level as any other person before or after him.

There's more. We can't find anyone else in history who even remotely came close to making similar claims about himself. What is declared about Jesus without any reservation is so consistently high, so extravagant, and so staggering that the only way we can regard him on the same level as others is to reject the assertions made about him. The only way we can reject those assertions is to have some defensible reason to do so, and the only way we can legitimately do so is to raise some questions that can't be satisfactorily answered by the evidence.

One initial, common objection can be dismissed immediately. It makes no sense whatsoever to complain that the concept of Jesus' uniqueness is "too narrow." How can an idea be narrow? As the great British thinker of the last century G. K. Chesterton taught us, an idea can't be narrow or broad. It can only be true or false. No idea can ever be broader than it is. So, narrow ideas simply don't exist.

Also, it doesn't work at all to say, as many do, "This has nothing to do with me. I have my own beliefs and Jesus is just not relevant to my life." But the only way this could be true would be if all his claims were untrue. For if they *were* true, to whom could they possibly be irrelevant? No one would fall outside the scope of them.

This would be somewhat like saying, "I don't have any personal investments, so the national economy has very little to do with my life. It makes no difference to me one way or the other." Some do think this way, but whether you are personally invested or not, the economic trends will have an impact upon the lives of every one of us.

What happens to the national economy will determine our employment or lack of it, the acceptance or rejection of our home loan, prices in the shoe store or supermarket, airfares, retirement plans, wage and salary increases, and a whole list of other things that do have a direct impact upon us. That's just the way the world is. We may not like it, but it is that way. Facts are facts.

In a much more profound and far-reaching sense, if Jesus is who he is claimed to be in the New Testament, then every person of every land and every time in history will be directly affected by him today and forever. He is the central figure of history, the determining factor for every single person's eternal destiny. His life, death, resurrection, ascension, ongoing reign with God the Father, and final return will, in the end, be the main events of all time. No one in any village of any nation, living in any remote part of the globe or far distant past, will be overlooked in the working out of God's eternal purpose.

It follows logically, then, and is not unreasonable in the slightest to say that this Jesus is not just another religious hero of the past – he is the only way to God and sole means of salvation. Of course, if this extravagant claim were made about anyone else, there would be plenty of room for skepticism.

Moreover, if (for the moment, theoretically) Jesus really was the person he and his followers claimed, what more could he have said than what he apparently did say? What more crystal clear language could he have used to convince us?

But let's slow down a bit. Let's walk more cautiously through the steps to see if these remarkable claims about Jesus should be taken seriously or tossed out altogether. We'll return to an earlier example.

As with the physical forces, what information can be assembled to put this question in proper perspective? First, we need to come to some conclusion as to whether Jesus really did make all these claims. Did Jesus actually say that apart from him there is no hope of eternal salvation, or was this statement merely something his enthusiastic but misguided followers made later on his behalf?

Surely, if there is no reason to believe that the assertions came from Jesus himself – that they're all purely fabrication and legend – then we need not go beyond this point. We can simply chalk them up to just another mistake on the part of well-meaning pious folk or even the sleight of hand of a group of slick religious charlatans.

Why Would Jesus' Followers Make False Claims?

From the point of view of plain common sense, it seems impossible to believe that his followers would make such claims if Jesus himself did not. What would be the point? The first disciples of Jesus were routinely accused, persecuted, hunted down, beaten, mercilessly tortured, ostracized from their communities, homes, families, and friends, and even brutally murdered for claiming to be associated with him.

It would be impossible to think that those martyrs who were eye- and ear-witnesses to the events of Jesus' life would deliberately fabricate a lie for which to suffer and die. It runs counter to all that we know of human behavior to assume that great numbers of people would create a fantastic fable about their leader, without any good reason for doing so, which would put themselves and their families in so much jeopardy.

Ironically, it was relatively common for those believers being murdered to utter things like, "May God have mercy upon you," or, "Lord, please don't hold this to their account," or a similar caring sentiment as they died. They often gave evidence that Jesus was in some sense there with them as they breathed their last.

We can easily imagine people suffering for a lie when they sincerely think it's the truth. This is a commonplace in every generation. History is full of instances where sincere followers believed their cause was true, only to find out later that they had been duped. But it's much more difficult to find cases where large numbers of people who concoct a lie are willing to sacrifice and die for it. Can you think of any?

Why would the great number of disciples fabricate so scandalous a claim? They could have easily asserted only that Jesus was just "another way" to salvation. The world of that day would have been all too happy (as is our world today) to celebrate one more claim to salvation among the many already on the market.

If ever there was a century like ours, with its bewildering variety of religious claims and options, it was the century in which the Gospel of Jesus was first proclaimed. Ours is not the first era which could be called the "Age of Pluralism." Far from it. In the days of Jesus and his followers, there were more religious choices available to the average person than there are varieties of ice cream today. Belief systems were everywhere abundant (read Acts 17). Just as we welcome one more flavor of ice cream, so the world of Jesus' and Paul's day would have been very receptive to one more system to add to the collection.

A curious incident recorded in Acts gives us a clue to what the intellectual environment was like in many of the cities of those days. Luke tells us that when Paul and his associates were walking through the streets of Philippi, a young woman began to follow them:

Once when we were going to the place of prayer, we were
met by a slave girl who had a spirit by which she predicted
the future. She earned a great deal of money for her owners
by fortune-telling. This girl followed Paul and the rest of us,
shouting, "These men are servants of the Most High God,
who are telling you the way to be saved." She kept this up for
many days. Finally Paul became so troubled that he turned
around and said to the spirit, "In the name of Jesus Christ
I command you to come out of her!" At that moment the
spirit left her.

Acts 16:16–18

The Greek grammar seems to suggest that what the
woman was actually crying out was that Paul and his party
were proclaiming in Jesus *one more* way ("a way") of salvation
among the many already offered. This would have been no
problem to the hearers in Philippi, for they were used to
hearing about new and intriguing religious systems. But this
was decidedly not what the Christians wanted said about
their Gospel, and Paul was quick to put a stop to it. The bold,
exclusive claims of Jesus are what got him crucified.[1]

All the Evidence Points in Another Direction

All available documentary evidence points to the fact
that Jesus himself claimed to be the unique revealer of God
and the only way to salvation. There has never been a single
convincing argument from skeptical scholars to the effect that
this feature was added after the fact by the creative adoration
of the church.

It runs through each and every stratum of evidence that
can be analyzed. We find it in the very earliest documents
of the church, namely, the writings of the Apostle Paul, in
the so-termed Synoptic Gospels (Matthew, Mark, and Luke),

as well as in the very different and independent Gospel of John. It stands even in the hypothetical source "Q" (material which occurs in Matthew and Luke, but not in Mark), which has been the object of much discussion in academic circles in the last several decades. This claim permeates the entire New Testament record and gives no hint of being tacked on later to more original information about Jesus.

Dating of the Manuscripts

It's obvious that the dates these documents were written would be profoundly important. If they were composed late – say, long after the death of the first witnesses – then we would be confronted by an entirely different historical problem. Who knows what kinds of distortions might have crept into the text of the New Testament? Without the control over the material by those who were on the scene of the events described in the ministry of Jesus, virtually any sort of fabrication or exaggeration could have found its way into the documents. This accusation is exactly what we are likely to hear in the "Bible as Literature" course in the average college or university.

But such objections carry no historical weight. Zero. None. They can be tested. Anyone, follower or skeptic, who has ever taken the time to look deeply into the facts of the case has discovered that many academic professionals, both believers and doubters, have arrived at a much different conclusion. It's common to find competent authorities stating that the date at which the New Testament came to its essential completion was well within the lifetime of the original eye- and ear-witnesses. Typically, the history of New Testament textual research confirms that the more we discover, the earlier we set the dates.

Even the renowned skeptical scholar John A. T. Robinson, made famous in the mid-twentieth century for his public rejection of many essentials of the Gospel, concluded that the New Testament was substantially completed by AD 70, firmly within the life spans of the first witnesses to the works and words of Jesus and his disciples.

When Robinson's book *Redating the New Testament* first appeared in 1976, it stunned the academic world because many scholars were expecting him to say what other intellectuals and theological liberals were saying. He would have been labeled a "fundamentalist" for writing his book had he not already become famous for being a skeptic. No one was quite sure what to say about him, so most just remained silent. But Robinson only confirmed what conservative scholars had been saying for many years. He wrote with no particular axe to grind about traditional Christian faith. As many before him, he simply followed where the historical evidence plainly led him.

It's worth noting that just six years before his death, he penned a little-known book entitled *Can We Trust the New Testament?* There, in the full fruition of a lifetime of highly detailed investigation of New Testament minutiae, he gave a very positive final verdict on its historical reliability (see Appendix C).

William Foxwell Albright (1891–1971), Professor of Semitic Languages at Johns Hopkins University, was known as the dean of biblical archeologists. He began his career highly doubtful of the Bible and its historicity. His theological liberalism faded with each year that he delved into the facts. After a long life of careful and critical study of the data, he made the following observation:

> In my opinion, every book of the New Testament was written by a baptized Jew between the forties and the eighties of

the first century AD (very probably between about AD 50 and 75).[2]

These conclusions would mean that most of the original eyewitnesses to the life and teaching of Jesus were still around to say whether or not something claimed for him was historically accurate. Just as important as the presence of the friendly witnesses, the original hostile witnesses would still be alive and more than ready to refute the claims of the believers. Far more enemies than friends of the new faith in Jesus were present. They would have been quick to counter or smother any claims that might add credibility to the sudden and shocking rise in the number of fully convinced believers in Jesus.

If for some reason (there are no good ones) we were to reject all this and accept the most skeptical and late dates for some of the New Testament writings, we would still be on firm historical ground for believing that the essentials of the Gospel story are intact. Virtually every scholar accepts as genuine most of the letters of Paul, who remains the earliest source of the facts of the primitive church. In the forms of early creeds, and perhaps hymns, he preserves in his writings some of the highest and most extravagant claims about Jesus known in the first century.

Many critical historians tend to rule out four of the thirteen letters of Paul, but even if we eliminate from consideration Ephesians, Colossians, First and Second Timothy (there are no compelling reasons for doing so), we are still left with the most weighty of the letters.

So there are no grounds for thinking that the bulk of the writings of the New Testament come to us any later than AD 70. While searching for a dissertation topic for my doctoral studies in New Testament, I settled on one that involved the letter of Second Peter. I was interested in this short letter for two reasons. First, it was considered by most scholars the latest writing in the New Testament, some assigning it to a period as late as the second century. Second, it was the leading candidate for being a *pseudepigraph* (a writing under a false name). I figured if this, the strongest case for a late-dated pseudepigraphical writing, was weak, then the lesser cases in the New Testament were no longer the serious challenge to the reliability and trustworthiness of the entire collection they were reputed to be.

I carried out my work in a secular university under the tutelage of a world authority on the letters of Peter, Swedish professor Bo Reicke, and under the fierce inspection of Swiss professor Markus Barth, who let me know early on that he would tolerate no Sunday School "Kinderspiel" (child's play) when it came to the final product.

I had to read virtually everything ever written about the letter of Second Peter. What I expected to find and what I actually did find were light years apart. The case for deliberate falsification of authorship for Second Peter, or any other New Testament writing, faded away. Moreover, there was not a single persuasive argument for its late dating. I had purposely kept my mind open on these issues, because it was the truth and nothing but the truth that I wanted. If the evidence had led in another direction, I would have followed it. My personal view of the Bible did not dictate how the search should come out.

This is what I discovered. Every argument for a very late writing by someone far removed from the circle of eyewitnesses depended entirely upon an eccentric interpretation of a few phrases in the text. This interpretation was forced upon it by a particular theory regarding early church history which was itself highly suspicious. The theory argues that Jesus' failure to return to earth during the disciples' lifetime caused a great theological crisis in the early church which embarrassed believers were forced to explain. If one doesn't share this view of early Christian history, then there is not the slightest reason to buy into the skeptical view of Second Peter.

In fact, New Testament students discover that there are as many "politically correct" views in theological study as in any other field. These views depend not so much upon the evidence, wherever it may lead, but upon prior commitments to certain assumptions and philosophies about "what we are prepared to accept." The school of naturalism, as outlined earlier, raises its proud head high in the field of biblical and theological study. Consequently, if students desire to be "successful" in the academic world, then by and large they should be prepared to fall in line with the "correct" conclusions of the day.

To summarize, the dating of the New Testament manuscripts presents serious problems only for those who are wishing them to be there. If we were dealing with any other documents of the ancient world, the difficulties would not even be mentioned.

But Can We Know That the Documents Really Are Trustworthy?

The only way we could believe that Jesus actually claimed to be the only way to God and the sole means of eternal salvation is to accept the idea that the documents containing that assertion really are accurate. The question is inescapable: Are they truly reliable representations of the life and message of Jesus? If it could be shown that these central documents are unreliable accounts of what they attempt to report, or that they are fraught with serious historical or documentary problems, then we would be walking on shaky ground to say that Jesus made the claim in the first place.

Fortunately, this is not a question recently introduced on the scene. It is all well-plowed ground, the subject of massive investigation for generations by many highly capable people. The issue has driven numerous investigators, including hardline skeptics, into this field of research. Many of them testify that they came to faith in Jesus Christ by pursuing this question to the end and being persuaded by the results.

You may consult any one of numerous works on the topic of New Testament reliability, but I'll summarize very briefly the results of widespread research.[3] First, consider the number of manuscripts available for investigation. If we compare the New Testament manuscripts with those of other writers which have survived from the ancient world, the New Testament comes out head and shoulders above them all. Scholars who study the writings of the Greek and Latin classical authors (e.g., Herodotus, Plato, Sophocles, Thucydides, Homer, Ovid, Cicero, and the like) discover that these literary and historical works, spoken of with such confidence in the university classroom, are typically based upon a mere hundred or so documents, or even as few as one or two.

Look at the following manuscript count for key classical writers:[4]

Homer: 643
Sophocles: 193
Caesar, *Gallic Wars*: 10
Aristotle: 49
Livy, *Roman History*: 35
Thucydides: 8
Tacitus, *Histories*: 4.5; *Annals*: 12
Suetonius: 8
Herodotus: 8
Plato: 7

The student who reads these ancient writers is rarely, if ever, told that the documentary evidence for the writers' thoughts is sometimes very scanty indeed. But even if this information is revealed, it is quickly pointed out that the science of textual criticism is so advanced that the problem of so few surviving manuscripts isn't a serious one. This is true. However, this is exactly one of those areas where criticism is often directed toward the New Testament. So the impression is created that while the other classical writers may be studied with complete confidence, the same does not hold true for the primary documents of the Christian faith.

A simple comparison of the evidence will dispel this devoutly held myth. In contrast to the documents which have survived for the classical Greek and Latin writers, the student of the New Testament faces the monumental task of working through not a mere handful or even a few hundred manuscripts, but literally thousands. There are well over 5,000 Greek manuscripts of the New Testament which have come down to us, creating not the problem of too little evidence to work with, but too much! If you add to that amount all the other manuscripts and versions of the Bible in other languages, such as Latin, Syriac, and so forth, the number of ancient documents swells to over 14,000. Include the many smaller fragments of available manuscripts and the number is even greater.

Incidentally, there are no parallels in manuscript evidence for any of the primary documents of the world's great religions. In this respect, the Bible stands alone.

As for the overall reliability of these documents, compared to all the other ancient writings, the case gets even stronger. Every ancient manuscript is faced with what is called the "gap problem." This means that there is a time gap between the actual time of writing and the date of the oldest surviving manuscript. Because no actual original manuscript (autograph) ever survived the ravages of time, we depend entirely upon copies of originals or even copies of copies. This is true for all ancient literature which is dependent upon written manuscripts rather than upon stone inscriptions and the like.

Let's say a particular classical writer composed his work around 350 BC, but the only surviving manuscript is dated around AD 1050. This would mean that a gap of 1,400 years exists between the time of actual writing and the surviving manuscript closest to that date. For the classical writers in general, this gap is often well over a thousand years.

Take a look at some typical time gaps:[5]

> Homer: 500 years
> Caesar: 1,000 years
> Demosthenes: 1,200 years
> Plato: 1,300 years
> Aeschylus, Aristophanes, Sophocles, Thucydides, and
>   Aristotle: 1,400 years
> Euripides: 1,600 years

When the professor of classical literature is quizzed about this time gap, his response is that this is not much of a problem. In light of all we now know about the field of textual criticism of ancient documents, we don't need to be in much doubt about whether or not we're getting a credible record of the ancient writer's work. The professor would be right. All things being equal, hundreds of years elapsing between the time of original writing and the oldest surviving manuscript of that writing are not seen as an issue serious enough to cast doubt on its essential historicity.

Yet again, this is precisely one of those areas cited in universities across the land as a huge, even fatal, weakness of the New Testament evidence for Jesus. But once more, the strength of the biblical manuscript evidence exceeds that of any of the ancient writings.

In our documents of the Christian faith, there's a gap not of a thousand years or more, but only a few hundred years – in some instances, just a short span of years. In the case of the Apostle John, for example, we have a manuscript fragment dated around the first quarter of the second century (circa AD 125), a mere handful of years from the original composition.

After a lifetime of work with ancient manuscripts, Sir Frederic G. Kenyon, formerly director and principal librarian of the British Museum, makes these remarks regarding the New Testament:

> In no other case is the interval of time between the composition of the book and the date of the earliest extant manuscripts so short as in that of the New Testament. The books of the New Testament were written in the latter part of the first century; the earliest extant manuscripts (trifling scraps excepted) are of the fourth century – say, from 250 to 300 years later.[6]

Elsewhere, Kenyon concludes:

> The interval then between the dates of original composition and the earliest extant evidence becomes so small as to be in fact negligible, and the last foundation for any doubt that the Scriptures have come down to us substantially as they were written has now been removed. Both the *authenticity* and the *general integrity* of the books of the New Testament may be regarded as finally established.[7]

Again, the New Testament comes out far and away superior in this respect to all ancient Greek or Latin literature.

An added confirmation which the New Testament

enjoys is the verification of those now known as the "Church Fathers," who wrote during the gap period about the New Testament, the church, and Christian theology, extensively quoting the Old and New Testaments. Students of theology will recognize names such as St. Ignatius, Polycarp, Irenaeus, Justin Martyr, Athanagoras, and the like. These men, so thoroughly steeped in the knowledge of the Scriptures, either directly quoted or alluded to so many passages in the Bible that virtually the entire New Testament could be reconstructed from their quotes and allusions alone.[8]

Thus, even if we did not possess a single manuscript of the New Testament itself – if not one of the 14,000 or so manuscripts had survived the ancient world – we would still possess the essence of the Gospels and letters preserved within the citations of the Fathers. This dramatic and thorough corroboration of the texts is not available in the study of Greek and Latin writings.

We should include one more confirmation of the New Testament writings, namely, the many discoveries in archeology which validate the written record. This includes the numerous tablets, monuments, inscriptions, and plates which have been unearthed to tell their story of people and events in the world of the New Testament.

It is beyond dispute today that the study of archeology has been a good friend of the Bible. Skeptics who had begun their work believing that the Bible was full of legends and tales ended their research with far different conclusions. One of history's greatest archeologists, Oxford professor Sir William Ramsay, actually went to Palestine to debunk the biblical record and came home a staunch believer. He recalls his early motivation and work in the following statement:

> I may fairly claim to have entered on this investigation without prejudice in favour of the conclusion which I shall now

seek to justify to the reader. On the contrary, I began with a mind unfavorable to it...but more recently I found myself brought into contact with the Book of Acts as an authority for the topography, antiquities, and society of Asia Minor. It was gradually borne upon me that in various details the narrative showed marvelous truth. In fact, beginning with a fixed idea that the work was essentially a second century composition, and never relying on its evidence as trustworthy for first century conditions, I gradually came to find it a useful ally in some obscure and difficult investigations.[9]

In the words of Yale University's archeologist Millar Burrows:

Archeological work has unquestionably strengthened confidence in the reliability of the scriptural record. More than one archeologist has found respect for the Bible increased by the experience of excavation in Palestine.[10]

The noted archeologist Nelson Glueck couldn't agree more:

It may be stated categorically that no archeological discovery has ever controverted a single biblical reference. Scores of archeological findings have been made which confirm in clear outline or in exact detail historical statements in the Bible.[11]

What about the information contained in the biblical manuscripts? Is it accurate? Can it stand up under fire from historians? Upon careful study, we find in this "internal evidence" the same quality and abundance of confirmation as we do in the "external evidence." Not a single historical or archeological discovery has provided a factual basis that would erode a student's confidence in the New Testament. Generally, the opposite has occurred. Historical references that scholars doubted generations ago have been more than confirmed by newer discoveries. The most famous and capable scholars in this field have been won over by the Bible's essential reliability.

A good test case for the New Testament's dependability is that of the Gospel writer Luke. Standing apart from all the others in this one respect, Luke takes the greatest risk of being proven wrong and opens himself to rigorous critique of his work's historical accuracy. More than any other New Testament writer, he includes so many precise historical references in his two-volume work (Luke and Acts) that historians can subject his work to the microscope of their investigations. They can inspect his references to dates, names, local religious and political leaders, events, rulers of the empire, and so forth.

When his writings were first examined by modern historians, he was criticized for creating nonexistent places and names, because they couldn't be verified elsewhere. However, after a century or so of further archeological discovery, he has been vindicated as a highly reliable historian of the first century. Here is Ramsay's verdict on Luke's work:

> Luke is a historian of the first rank; not merely are his statements of fact trustworthy; he is possessed of the true historic sense; he fixes his mind on the idea and plan that rules in the evolution of history, and proportions the scale of his treatment to the importance of each incident.... In short, this author should be placed along with the very greatest of historians.[12]

Ramsay added to this assessment:

> Luke's history is unsurpassed in respect of its truthworthiness.[13]

The classical historian A. N. Sherwin-White corroborated Ramsay's work regarding the book of Acts:

> Any attempt to reject its basic historicity even in matters of detail must now appear absurd. Roman historians have long taken it for granted.[14]

Yet we frequently hear that the New Testament record is fraught with manuscript and historical discrepancies. If we were to base our conclusions on what we hear in the local college classroom or on television, we would be sure that the New Testament is so full of problems that no thinking person would ever take it seriously. The truth is that if serious doubt is cast on the reliability of these documents, then the entire university system of ancient history and classical studies needs to be shut down, for if the stronger case is to be thrown out, the weaker case has no hope of survival. We should never again hear a quote of any ancient Greek or Roman writer coming from the areas of history, philosophy, or literature.

On the other hand, if the weaker case (the classics) has been vindicated as historically reliable (which it has), then the stronger case (the New Testament) enjoys the vastly superior position. The believer doesn't have to apologize for putting confidence in the writings we know as the "Testament of our Lord and Savior Jesus Christ." Skeptics are invited to examine with all their energy the massive data that lies beneath and behind the faith of the Christian church. Perhaps the New Testament is more reliable than our postmodern media!

Were the Claims Merely an Example of "Legend"?

We all are aware of how legends grow. First, some great event takes place or an extraordinary person appears on the scene. Some time later, the story begins to change. Then, as it is told and retold, the events get blown way out of proportion to their original size. The person is elevated over time to a position far above their actual importance, power, or abilities. Occasionally, this happens even during a person's lifetime. (Some writers refer to "true legends" or "true myths," but most people understand these terms to mean fables or fairy tales. For us now, the use of these words corresponds to this popular meaning.)

The more time that elapses, the higher the claims get. A famous baseball player, a great statesman, or a powerful religious figure can come to be viewed as almost superhuman as the story is heightened over decades or centuries. In fact, tracing the origin and development of a legend is much like *descending* a mountain. The stature of a legendary person gets smaller and more proportionate as you get closer to the historical roots. The more reliable information we discover about the person in question, the more they appear just like ourselves — full of flaws, inconsistencies, and weaknesses typical of what we know to be human.

Following the trajectory of a legend in religious history is often a fairly simple matter. For example, Islamic tradition is full of miraculous accounts of its prophet, Muhammad. However, the Koran is very clear on this subject. There is no claim whatsoever in the text that the Arabian prophet ever performed a miracle or that Muhammad himself ever professed to have such powers. Islamic scholars are careful to point out that the Koran openly disclaims such powers on the part of its leader. Nevertheless, in direct contradiction to the text, the later traditions surrounding the religious leader elevate him to a legendary worker of miracles.

We can even observe how legends developed around the names of the Apostle Paul and the other apostles. Long after their deaths, fiction writers appeared on the scene (during the second through fourth centuries AD) to fill in the historical blanks with fantastic stories about them. No church authority ever seriously entertained the idea that these were anything other than legends.

Legends about Jesus arose long after the first century passed, following the same predictable lines. They made for interesting and entertaining reading, but their portrayals of the young Jesus as a supernatural wonderboy were of no use to the church in arriving at the truth about Jesus' life and teaching.

What is interesting about these late legends is that they did not increase Jesus' stature or status from the earlier genuine accounts of him. There was nothing left to elevate. The first reports of him were already so extravagant and off the charts that there was no way to make them any higher. If anything, legends which began to develop about Jesus in the century after his death *diminished* his status or character.

The exact opposite of legendary development is observed when doing historical investigation about the person of Jesus. The closer you get to the original Jesus, the greater the person. Approaching the person of Jesus historically is like *ascending* a mountain. As you get closer and closer to the person himself, the claims appear higher and higher.

Since it is almost universally agreed today, even among skeptics, that the earliest documentary evidence about Jesus and the primitive church comes from the genuine writings of the Apostle Paul, it is there we find some of the first and highest claims about him. Earlier still are those traditions about Jesus which Paul cites in his letters that come in the form of what are thought to be either hymns sung by Christians or creeds recited by them years before Paul's conversion.

One noted example is found in his first letter to the church at Corinth where he summarizes the essential features of Christian belief handed down to him by those who had come to faith before him:

Now, brothers, I want to remind you of the gospel I preached to you, which you received and on which you have taken your stand. By this gospel you are saved, if you hold firmly to the word I preached to you. Otherwise, you have believed in vain. For what I received I passed on to you as of first importance: that Christ died for our sins according to the Scriptures, that he was buried, that he was raised on the third day according to the Scriptures, and that he appeared to Peter, and then to the Twelve.

1 Corinthians 15:1–5

Another possible example occurs in Paul's letter to the church at Philippi:

Who, being in very nature God,
     did not consider equality with God something
          to be grasped,
but made himself nothing,
     taking the very nature of a servant,
     being made in human likeness.
And being found in appearance as a man,
     he humbled himself
and became obedient to death –
     even death on a cross!
Therefore God exalted him to the highest place
     and gave him the name that is above every name,
that at the name of Jesus every knee should bow,
     in heaven and on earth and under the earth,
and every tongue confess that Jesus Christ is Lord,
     to the glory of God the Father.

Philippians 2:6–11

In both instances, Paul is incorporating into his letters those earlier pieces of widely accepted information. In the case of the Philippians reference, Paul is describing Jesus in the highest possible terms, embodying the highest Christology known in the early church. No more lofty claim could be made about Jesus than that he descended from his pre-earthly, heavenly existence to become a servant, deliberately taking the form of human flesh.

While some scholars have thought this section (Philippians 2) to be a Christian hymn sung by early believers, others have surmised that it was a creed recited in corporate worship. No one knows for sure. What seems certain is that it existed prior to Paul's writing and is something he had received. In any case, it reflects both a very early description and, at the same time, one of the very highest statements of who Jesus was and what he came to do.[15]

Another important source of these expressions of faith in Jesus is the section of the so-called "speeches" of Acts, particularly in the first fifteen chapters. These condensed summaries of early Christian thought and preaching appear to have been handed down through the years and then recorded by Luke, who acted as the researcher and compiler of written and/or oral sources of information. He was attempting to preserve the most historically reliable information possible about Jesus and the church in order to persuade and encourage a high-ranking intellectual named Theophilus (Luke 1:1–4; Acts 1:1). In so doing, Luke used the best methods and techniques of history writing known at the time.[16]

A further possible example known among scholars of this incorporation of earlier material into the text is from the prologue of John's Gospel:

> In the beginning was the Word, and the Word was with God, and the Word was God. He was with God in the beginning. Through him all things were made; without him nothing was made that has been made. In him was life, and that life was the light of men.
>
> John 1:1–4

No one can be completely sure, but based on its literary characteristics, many have thought that verses one through four were part of an early Christian hymn, or perhaps a simple baptismal creed recited by the worshippers of Jesus.

In the centuries to follow, the church's battle was to keep the claims of Jesus as high as they originally were. When new heresies arose, they typically functioned to lower the claims to a more comfortable level, not raise them. Some tried to de-emphasize Jesus' humanity while others tried to downplay his deity because one aspect or the other was deemed offensive to a particular heretical group.

The natural tendency within both religious and pagan circles was to find the exceedingly high claims of Jesus repugnant. They could not be raised any higher than they already were, so there really was only one way to go – down. If you start with the highest of all possible claims – that, among other things, Jesus Christ is the preexistent co-Creator, Lord of history, standard of the final judgment, and destiny of the entire human race (see Appendix A) – where do you go from there?

Even Legends Have Their Limits

How do you start with a human being (even an extraor-dinary one) and arrive at the astonishing heights to which the New Testament carries us? Jesus is regarded as Lord of lords, King of kings, eternal Son of God, and one with God the Father, who alone discloses who the Creator is and what He wants, who alone embodies and fulfills the earthly and eternal purposes of God.

Even in his lifetime he was worshipped by those who knew him best. No progressive development would have led his disciples to worship him as God for the obvious reason that they were Jews who had a radical commitment to monotheism and, as the Romans discovered, possessed an extreme abhorrence of worshipping humans as gods. This factor alone would have worked against any such legend developing within the Jewish-Christian community.

It doesn't really matter whether you're reading from the letters of Paul, Peter, James, or from the Gospels. The same high view of Jesus is preserved throughout the New Testament. The only way to deny these claims in the text is either to create homemade historical criteria for their acceptability or ignore them altogether.

Not long ago, a world-renowned biblical critic was being interviewed by a well-known TV news personality. The man was asked about the famous claim Jesus makes in the Gospel of John: "I am the way and the truth and the life. No one comes to the Father except through me" (John 14:6). The "scholar" responded that since this claim cannot be found in any of the other Gospels, we aren't required to take it seriously. It was just a quirk, an exception to the rule, preserved in one of the very latest writings of the New Testament. He went on to argue that we should not accept anything that appears in the Bible only once, particularly of a legendary nature.

What the interviewer didn't know, and what the speaker failed to disclose, is that even though these exact words do not appear outside the Gospel of John, the exact same thought occurs in all the Gospels and in the letters which predated them.

Let's recap what was mentioned earlier:

- All things are committed to Jesus by God. No one knows the Son except the Father and no one knows the Father except the Son and those to whom Jesus chooses to reveal Him (Matthew 11:27).

- Jesus calls God his "Abba" ("Daddy" or "Papa"). No other Jew in history ever dared use such intimate language about the Creator (Mark 14:36).

- No one comes to a knowledge of God unless Jesus grants permission (Luke 10:22).

Remember, too, the many statements about Jesus preserved by those circles of disciples who knew him best (see earlier list of references and Appendix A).

If it be objected that Jesus was not who he said he was but merely a deluded fanatic, it must at least be admitted that those who came closest to him believed he was the incarnate and resurrected Lord, Son of God, and only Savior of the world. If the assertions of later generations attempted to demote him, it was because there were many in the ancient world who wanted very much to diminish belief in him. But all this is decidedly not how a legend develops.

If the skeptics of today consider Jesus simply a human being who was later elevated to divine status, then it could be argued that they have fallen for an account of him which should be classified as a legend in reverse, a slow and steady reduction of his status. They are on the losing end of a centuries-long decline in his reputation.

Limits of History

There are also limits to historical investigation. The study of history is done on probabilities. Whether you're looking into the life of Julius Caesar or Jesus Christ, you are limited to your own sources and interpretation of what probably happened. What is argued here is that if we study the life and ministry of Jesus with all the same methods as any other figure of the past, we can be at least as sure of the portrait of Jesus as virtually any other person in ancient history.

From the historical information available to us, we know far more about Jesus than we do about many other figures of the ancient world whom we routinely mention in our conversations. This doesn't mean that the New Testament tells us everything we want to know, nor does it imply that there are no problems or difficulties associated with the sources. What all the above means is that whenever we ask good historical questions about the documents, we get good historical answers. It also lets the believer match stride for stride the challenges of the skeptic, and even come out on top.

Parenthetically, it may be added that for believers in Jesus, historical probability is not the only grounds for our knowledge of and connection to the Son of God. The church has long maintained that if Jesus really did rise from the dead on Easter morning, then he is still alive and therefore accessible to his followers. Most sincere believers in Jesus admit to having some real contact with him in the present through answered prayer, dramatic rescues, healings, divine direction, coincidental events, reading Scripture, the corporate life of the church, and the like. Nevertheless, historical investigation is still vital in demonstrating that what we experience in the present can be supported by historical facts. This means that true faith is still firmly rooted in fact, regardless of the present experiences of Jesus we may have.

In the end, whatever we choose to think of the information that has come down to us about Jesus Christ, we can't argue successfully that it follows the typical pattern of legend building.

A Note on the Human Jesus

The hidden assumption behind this view that Jesus was just a man who was later elevated to divine status is that there's something innately "low" about being human. It is supposed that if Jesus showed himself as fully human, then he couldn't have shared in any way the nature and character of the "Father," the Creator of the universe. It is further reasoned (falsely) that any evidence in the New Testament of Jesus' humanity should be found in the earliest layers of tradition, while the claims of deity or unique relationship to the Father would naturally be found in the later.

However, this low view of humanity has little to do with the biblical view of things. The Bible's understanding of what it means to be human is quite different from ours. In the Old Testament it already appears that a human being is something quite wonderful and majestic. In the creation narrative of Genesis (chapters 1 and 2), it is clear that everything God made (particularly human beings) was good. In fact, it is emphasized that His entire creation was "very good" (1:31). The crown of God's creative work was the human being.

Psalm 8, for example, reiterates that human beings are so marvelous in their design that they were made "little less than God" – an exaggeration to be sure, but a bold statement of the incomparable glory of the human creation. In other words, there was nothing "merely" about being created human. It was considered extremely high to bear the very image of God.

We are like survivors of a majestic ship carrying royalty which sank on its maiden voyage at the dawn of creation. When we washed up on the beach with seaweed in our hair, clothes torn, bruised and battered, we didn't look much like royalty, but we were. It was up to Jesus to search us out, find us marooned on a hostile island far from home, and carry us back to our homeland to rule the kingdom with him.

To consider Jesus as the human incarnation of God was not to build a legend, but to say that God had a very high evaluation of His creation and thought that sending His Son into the world as a real man was an extremely good thing. In so doing, God intended to reveal to us in living color what He is like as well as to demonstrate to us fallen creatures what a real human being is supposed to be like. He expected His image to be manifested in His human creations just as He designed. The coming of God's Son into flesh and blood was to be the beginning of a radical reconstruction of what had been lost in the Fall.

Jesus Christ of Nazareth, therefore, was not a Superman, but a man – a normal human. In comparison to him, we now dwell as *subhumans* waiting to become fully human one day. Our ultimate destiny is not to become gods or God, but to become human, in all the proportions and dimensions of the original divine intent (see question 15 in chapter five). So the more we learn about Jesus, the greater the scandal becomes. Not only is he the only way to God and ultimate salvation – he's also the only way to full humanity! Apart from him no one will ever reach it.

To sum it all up, it isn't possible to sort out the so-called "legendary" elements of the Gospel and pronounce which is the earliest view of Jesus Christ and which is the latest. Both the divine status and the full humanity of Jesus confront us at the very beginning of the Gospel and are repeated themes throughout the New Testament. We meet them both early and late. This dual nature of Jesus may be regarded as an *irreducible complexity*. This means that it cannot be made more simple than it already is. One attribute can't be seen as a later development of the other, nor can one be separated and analyzed without the other. They come as a complete, inseparable, and functioning whole from the start.

The New Testament invites us to explore something entirely new and unparalleled in history. It declares the arrival not of a man who over time came to be thought of as God, but God who took on human flesh and became a real man in real history. If this is true, then it would be utterly futile to attempt to apply a model of "development" which assumes from the start that it is not.

A Note on the Resurrection of Jesus

The New Testament affirms that Jesus Christ died a real death on Good Friday and was raised bodily from the grave on Easter morning. It is careful to reinforce the truth that the same body which was put into the grave after the crucifixion was the same body which came out of it. To be sure, it was a transformed body, but it was in substantial continuity with the Jesus of Nazareth who walked the earth just days before.

This resurrection from the dead was understood to be the ultimate and decisive vindication of Jesus' claims and validation of his identity and work. It wasn't a legend tacked on to the story of an extraordinary man, but the natural and promised conclusion to the life and work of the God-man. The resurrection, cited by all believers thereafter, was the confirmation that Jesus really was who he said he was and that he really had accomplished what he said he would.

He was the unique Son of God who had no equals in history. He came to live a human life and die a human death, and to absorb into himself all the consequences of our sin and folly. In other words, he came to pay a price for our salvation which we were not capable of paying.

What Adam in his disobedience failed to do, Jesus in his obedience succeeded in doing. The "first Adam" (1 Corinthians 15:45) rebelled and fell from his majestic status by trying to snatch the rights of God – to be his own god and determine for himself what is good, right, and true. On the other hand, Jesus Christ, the "last Adam" (1 Corinthians 15:45), the "heavenly human" (1 Corinthians 15:47), fulfilled the divine commission and led the fallen race back to their intended home.

What was it that demonstrated once and for all that this was true? The resurrection. Nothing short of the drama of the real, bodily resurrection from the dead would have justified his astonishing claims. Such an event would have been perfectly in line with and in exact proportion to the rest of his life. Without it, he would have been just another deluded zealot. There were plenty of them in his day.

It was Jesus' coming out of the tomb and appearing alive to hundreds of people (both followers and unbelievers alike) that propelled the first Christians around the known world with the good news. They declared fearlessly that since Jesus was evermore alive, death was now a defeated enemy and that life – not death – was God's last word to his creatures. His Easter morning defeat of death was the one central fact around which all the theology of the New Testament was organized.

Today many liberal theologians argue for a "spiritual resurrection." They assert that either Jesus' physical body remained in the tomb on Easter morning or it was devoured by wild dogs even before the first day of the week (the day of the resurrection), and that what motivated the earliest Christians was the mere idea that Jesus was still alive. But such a spiritual resurrection would have been of no interest to the first disciples. They were Jews. They could not have cared less about spirits coming back from the dead. For them, resurrection involved a physical body, or it was not a resurrection at all.

The resurrection of Jesus was physical all the way. The

New Testament spells out clearly that Jesus' post-resurrection appearances were not those of a ghost (Luke 24:36–39; John 20:26–27), but of a transformed physical body. It took this kind of resurrection to convince the disciples that what God had in mind in Jesus was not the "salvation of souls," but the restoration and redemption of the entire physical, material order (Romans 8:22–23). It was not "immortal souls" that mattered to God, but immortal bodies and an immortal creation that He originally made and always loved.

What is striking about Jesus' resurrection in the New Testament is that it is not argued *for*. It is always argued *from*. It's not the conclusion of an argument, but rather is consistently the premise of other arguments. It was the one issue squabbling believers, who argued about everything else under the sun, never debated – the one piece of history that was not in any doubt. It was the single, nonnegotiable, bedrock fact of faith. So surely was it established in the minds of the first eye- and ear-witnesses of Jesus that if it was not true, then nothing else was. For this, they were willing to risk all.

Jesus made sure before his ascension to the Father (Acts 1:1–3) that his disciples were not in the slightest doubt that their Lord was alive and would not and could not ever die. He would be with them to the end of the age (Matthew 28:9–10). Over a period of forty days, he gave them every personal proof desired that the physical resurrection was real. Various tests were provided for them: the sight test (multiple appearances), the sound test (multiple conversations), the touch or ghost test, and the continuity test (study Matthew 28; Luke 24; John 20 and 21; Acts 1; and 1 Corinthians 15:1–8).

It would not be true to say that he appeared only to the convinced. Rather, no one who witnessed his appearances remained unconvinced. His physical presence and post-resurrection activities thoroughly dispelled doubt and skepticism.

Because of this absolute surety of the resurrection of Jesus, the disciples allowed themselves to be mistreated, arrested, abused, tortured, and killed in order to get the message out that death had died and new life was possible for anyone who desired it. It was a free gift which could not be earned by any means whatsoever, but was available to those who would acknowledge sin, confess it, turn from it, and receive the gift of eternal life.

Of course, the resurrection would seem preposterous and out of proportion if it had been claimed about any of the disciples, or if it were now claimed about you or me. It would be as difficult to believe as the skeptics tell us it is. But since it was claimed for Jesus of Nazareth, preexistent Son of God, it is in perfect accord with his nature, character, and purpose. He was the only human to hold authority over demonic powers, over every kind of sickness and malady, over weather, over molecules, and even over death itself. If the details of his identity and mission were true, then it would have been a surprise and entirely out of order for it not to happen.

It is beyond the scope of this book to provide a thorough defense of the resurrection of Jesus. Arguments for the resurrection are substantial and compelling, and many have come to faith simply by investigating it.[17] One Jewish historian, Pinchas Lapide, entirely rejects the claim that Jesus was the Messiah but believes that he rose from the dead on Easter morning because he finds the historical evidence for it convincing.[18]

A brief summary of the evidence for the resurrection corresponds to what are usually regarded as minimal requirements for an accurate historical account. Among them are:

- The sources reporting the events have some eye- and ear-witnesses behind them.

- The witnesses to the events are credible.

- The dates of the first accounts are within reasonable proximity to the events reported.

- Multiple accounts of the same event display some basic overlap or core of common information.

- Variations of detail exist among witnesses, since exact correspondence in every particular suggests collusion.

- Manuscripts are well attested and stand up under critical examination according to the usual criteria of historical and literary analysis.

- The historian's personal prejudices and passions are minimized in the interest of fair and equal application of historical criteria to manuscript evidence.

As these and other fundamental, commonsense principles are applied to the resurrection accounts in the New Testament, the foundation for confidence in the historicity of the resurrection of Jesus is established. When they are used to evaluate the reports of the earliest eye- and ear-witnesses, the evidence of the empty tomb, the position and condition of the grave clothes, the testimony of the appearances of Jesus over nearly a six-week period, the absence of any counter-testimony claiming to see the dead body of Jesus, and the ongoing presence of the risen Christ among his followers, we have every right to affirm the historical truth of the bodily resurrection of Jesus Christ.

It's the most investigated, inspected, analyzed, and debated event of all time. Yet professional historians and philosophers of every generation since the first century have found the evidence for the resurrection of Jesus compelling. Oxford philosopher Richard Swinburne concludes that when all the above evidence is put through the filter of up-to-date probability theory, the weight of probability is on the side of the traditional believer.[19]

The usual grounds for dismissing the historical claim are those of some prior commitment to a belief system (the faith of atheism) which categorically denies the possibility of such a miracle ever occurring. Such a denial is not an assertion of reason over faith, but simply indicates a quarrel between two different faiths.

3:
objections

"For Something This Important, We Need Far More Evidence"

An interesting objection to the reliability of the New Testament is this: "Okay, we've heard the case, but it's not good enough. In matters such as God, salvation, and eternal destiny, we need more evidence than usual to be convinced, since these issues are far more important than mere historical questions about emperors or wars. The evidence for the New Testament falls short."

This objection appears to be a convenient excuse or backup plan for someone who has challenged the historical reliability of the New Testament and been confronted with the fact that the documents stand head and shoulders above all other ancient literature. This protest sounds fairly reasonable. Should it carry any weight?

The answer could be both no and yes. First, if more evidence is required for the New Testament and the claims of Jesus than for other historical documents, then that should be stated upfront. We should hear it before, not after, the challenge has been made and met. This looks suspiciously like the little boy who dares his playmate to jump over a two-foot fence, then after he does, makes him jump a three-foot fence, and so on, and so forth. The bar is raised with each successive try.

When modern historical challenges are made to the New Testament, the challengers typically appear quite confident that no successful defense can be mounted to meet the high demands of more advanced historical investigation. After it's demonstrated beyond a reasonable doubt that the documents can not only meet but exceed the credentials of other ancient sources, they then object that the issues are too serious to take mere historical data as any sort of proof.

But it isn't considered "mere historical data" when the challenge is first made. Rather, the rigorous standards for attaining accurate historical information are usually considered the height of good sense and intellectual excellence under any circumstances. Great (even excessive) conviction is often maintained regarding the final results of the historian's work with the newly developed tools of research. So it's simply not very convincing or even fair-minded for one side to reverse field and attempt to change the rules in mid-game. Either they're good rules to follow, or they aren't. You have to decide.

Second, we can't ask more of history than it can give. There are limits to how much historical investigation can tell us. Whether we are talking about Julius Caesar or the Battle of Thermopylae, we rarely have all the information we want. Sometimes the data comes to us fully packed with facts we're not interested in, but very sparse in those areas we want to know a great deal more about. That's just the way historical sources are. Our expectations and questions are frequently greater than what the documents can supply. In such cases, we wait for more information or look to other areas of study to fill in the blanks.

Even though the objection is not entirely fair to impose upon any historical question, we may nevertheless have some personal sympathy with it. Admittedly, I do. When we're talking about such ultimate matters as the meaning of life and eternal destiny, I want a lot more, too! It's true that our eternal fate is far more important than anything related to the Battle of Thermopylae. It would be very unsatisfying and unconvincing to hear that we need to make a profound, life-altering decision about Jesus of Nazareth based purely upon some historical data. Faith in Jesus Christ isn't just intellectual assent to information about the ancient world. Far from it!

The case for faith in Jesus is not wholly controlled by historical research, as good as the results of that research are. According to the New Testament, it involves a fundamental transformation of the mind and heart as well as a sweeping reevaluation of all of life. It is closely tied to real history (it doesn't even make any sense without it!), but it isn't entirely explained by historical research. Genuine Christian faith entails multileveled proofs, requiring a highly personal transaction between our Creator and us, initiated and carried through by Him to its ultimate fulfillment – fully human, physical life in His presence forever (see *The Nature of Faith in Jesus*, page 117).

"It's Just a Matter of Interpretation"

This old favorite of homemade philosophy is one of the first objections we hear when stating that Jesus is the only way to God and salvation. "It's all in the way you interpret it," comes the sure reply. This qualification is somehow supposed to sort it all out for us. It is offered as a substitute for a full, rational explanation as if nothing more need be said about the whole business. Being now so steeped in the doctrine of "whateverism," we think that this stops the conversation. "Yes, I guess that's what it all comes down to," is the general consensus, accepting one person's spin on the subject as just as good as another's.

But take a closer look at this view. Let's say that we're sitting around the table with people of many different backgrounds and perspectives and are reading from John's Gospel:

> I am the way and the truth and the life. No one comes to the Father except through me.
>
> John 14:6

Next we turn to the Gospel of Luke:

> All things have been committed to me by the Father. No one knows who the Son is except the Father, and no one knows who the Father is except the Son and those to whom the Son chooses to reveal him.
>
> Luke 10:22

Now to the book of Acts:

> There is salvation in no one else. There is no other name under heaven given among men by which we must be saved.
>
> Acts 4:12

Following this, someone asks, "What do these statements mean and what is your interpretation of them?" How many options are there? When Jesus says that he is the way, the truth, and the life and that no one comes to God except through him, what do he and the writer of the Gospel want us to understand? When the apostles said that there is no other name under heaven by which we must be saved, what are we to deduce from that?

Let's assume that one participant says "Well, I think that there are many ways to God. These statements can be interpreted in other ways."

Okay. We may then respond, "What are the ways? Show us how this works out. Explain what other interpretations there are and how they might have been the writers' original intent." Keeping in mind that we may or may not like what the writers say by the statements, what did they intend for us to understand by them? If we depart from the so-called "original intent" rule, which has governed our interpretation of information for as long as there have been rules of logic, then we open ourselves up to some serious problems in communication.

Let me give a simple illustration. A university professor of Constitutional Law, lecturing his class on the American Constitution, says, "I want you to know that we are not bound by the original intent of the writers of the Constitution. What the Founders said in the Constitution and in the Declaration of Independence is not exactly what we are to understand today by these documents. It's all a matter of interpretation. The Constitution means what we say it means, not what the original writers intended. We must try to understand it from within our own current situation." (The professor is one who is termed a "loose constructionist.")

This notion may sound very high-toned and reasonable to some unsuspecting law student and is, in fact, the view being taught in many of today's law schools. But where does this lead us? What would happen if we applied this logic to the professor's own statements? What if each student in the class walked away from the lecture hall that morning with their own interpretation, determined entirely by each one's "current situation."

One of the students, Ralph, says, "You know, from what the professor was saying, I guess we don't need to try and figure out what he originally intended for us to understand from his lecture today."

Cindy agrees, "Yeah, I think we need to interpret his statements in terms of our own current situations."

Josh concludes, "Exactly – it's all just a matter of interpretation. I can think of several different meanings to the words he used this morning. I don't think we need to pay any attention to what he intended for us to understand way back at 9:00 a.m. I mean, come on, it's already noon – a new time!"

The professor would be very disturbed when he got back the exams at the end of the quarter with numerous personal and widely divergent interpretations of his lectures. The students would surely flunk the exam, but they would protest (rightly) that they were merely applying the guidelines for interpretation he himself gave them.

Clearly, this ideology of personal, subjective, and multiple interpretations is self-devouring. It eats itself up immediately after being presented.

What has happened in the study of the Constitution is closely paralleled in the study of Scripture and theology in many of our seminaries. Today, Scripture often means not what the original writer intended it to mean, but what the reader chooses it to mean "in light of our current situation." However, for most of those who passed through the halls of academia in generations past, what a statement really meant was simply the writer's intent. It could not mean any number of things unless it was so ambiguous or poorly written that it left itself open to anyone's interpretation.

If you remember studying Shakespeare in the classroom, the teacher was usually very intolerant of your own interpretation of a passage. The marginal notes tried to explain in minute detail what particular words and phrases meant in Shakespeare's day.

Or, if you remember trying to decipher a long-awaited

love letter, you probably tried with all your might to squeeze every last drop of original intent out of it. "What did she really mean by that?" When it comes to the daily business of communication – purchase orders, monthly bills, wills, insurance forms, home loan applications, letters from the Internal Revenue Service, even grocery lists – what is of first importance is not creative interpretation of them, but getting the point of the sender. If we don't, bad things happen!

So it is with reading the New Testament Gospels and letters. In truth, the Bible is undoubtedly the most examined, most analyzed, and most rigorously studied of any writing in history. It has undergone more textual criticism, more syntactical, grammatical, linguistic, and historical scrutiny than any other written text. It is put through more literary filters and looked at with more microscopic inspection by more people than any other literature ever composed. So in the vast majority of biblical texts, it is possible to determine with a high degree of precision what the original author intended to convey.

Biblical texts are studied not only by believers, but by skeptics, atheists, devotees of other religions, and even by those who haven't the slightest interest in whether the Bible is true or not. Regardless of our convictions, if we use the linguistic tools carefully, the meaning of most texts becomes clear. Some of the best books written about the works of the Apostle Paul, for instance, have been produced by people who didn't believe a word Paul wrote. But they did accurately preserve what Paul intended to say and what he wanted the reader to believe. The scholars were simply being faithful to the tools of their trade.

Thus the tattered phrase, "It's all a matter of interpretation," just doesn't do the job. Most who attempt to use this excuse are not able, when pressed, to defend it consistently. It's simply an easy out for those unwilling to face up to the serious implications of the words they read in the Bible.

"But Isn't This Just Like *Telephone*?"

It's surprising how many people object, "How can we trust something that has been passed from one person to another over many years? We all know from the kids' game *Telephone* that things get changed in transmission – what was said in the beginning comes out totally different in the end."

True. If this really was the way the New Testament accounts of Jesus and the apostles were transmitted from one person to another, or from one generation to another, we would have plenty to worry about. Fortunately, it has nothing to do with the way the Gospel material and information about the early church were preserved and passed along.

Telephone is what might be termed the "chain link" form of transmission, where the accuracy of information depends entirely upon the integrity of each link in the chain. Sometimes the facts put in at the beginning are deliberately changed to make the game more fun, and sometimes what is whispered to another is not clearly heard and is inadvertently misunderstood. What the last person says is often unrecognizable from the original message.

The New Testament (as well as the Old) was transmitted in an entirely different way, one which could be termed the "community" form of transmission. The difference between this and the "chain link" method can be illustrated by an experiment a pastor friend tried when he was in charge of a church group of about twenty youth. He brought two short news reports clipped from the local newspapers – one about a car accident, the other about a crime. Each report contained seven facts.

Then he took the first clipping and read it separately to one youth. He read it several times and stressed the importance of trying to memorize and pass on the seven facts as accurately as possible, emphasizing that this was no game. The first youth pulled the next person aside and repeated the story to them from memory. This continued until they all were given a chance to hear and repeat it. At the end, they recorded on a chalkboard the facts which survived the transmission. Of the seven facts, only one piece of information (and it was distorted at that!) survived.

Next the pastor took the second newspaper clipping and read it to the group as a whole. They were asked to reproduce as a group as many of the seven facts as possible. One person contributed one fact, another remembered accurately several items, and one even retained the entire seven. As a group working together – each one adding, correcting, and coaching one another to recall as accurately as possible – they preserved all seven facts without distortion.

This is not in any way suggested as a scientific proof of anything – only as a partial parallel to the way the New Testament has been passed on. The events, sayings, and conversations which have come to make up the New Testament were received, preserved, and passed on by a community of highly devout people.

This meant the original eye- and ear-witnesses were there to remember and preserve what they had seen and heard. Don't forget: not only were the friendly and believing recipients present, but the unbelieving and even hostile witnesses were still around to correct any false accounts given by the believers. Before these original witnesses passed from the scene and a new generation arose who had not seen or heard directly, the information was fixed in written form. As mentioned earlier, this is why the early dates of the documents are so important.

An additional fact adds weight to the credibility of this

process of transmission. Most of the first Christians and virtually all (except for maybe one) of the writers of the New Testament were Jewish. They were raised in Jewish homes, learned Jewish customs, and enjoyed Jewish culture and religion. A principal practice of the Jewish people, dating from ancient times and taken with extreme seriousness, was to commit to memory what they believed to be the very words of God – the Hebrew Scriptures.

From a very early age, Hebrew boys were trained to retain and pass on with extraordinary accuracy what they had been taught, either orally or by means of the written text. This was considered one of the highest things they could do in life. Professor Bernard Ramm explains this:

> Jews preserved as no other manuscript has ever been preserved. With their massora they kept tabs on every letter, syllable, word and paragraph. They had special classes of men within their culture whose sole duty was to preserve and transmit these documents with practically perfect fidelity.... Who ever counted the letters, syllables and words of Plato or Aristotle? Cicero or Seneca?[1]

Therefore, when these same people came to believe that they had found their Messiah in the Jew Jesus of Nazareth, they applied the same consummate skill of remembering and memorizing the deeds and words of their Lord as they had in internalizing and passing on those of the Old Testament Scriptures.

A fascinating test case was provided by the discovery of the Dead Sea Scrolls in 1947. No New Testament document was unearthed there, nor, as the evidence has since shown, was there much light shed on Jesus, the disciples, or the early church. But some Old Testament manuscripts were found among the writings of the sect which dwelt in the area.

Prior to that time, the closest Hebrew manuscript of the

prophet Isaiah anyone possessed was dated many centuries after his life in the eighth century BC. Many scholars believed, on the basis of other evidence, that the Hebrew Scriptures were highly accurate in their preservation and transmission. When a copy of the Isaiah Scroll from roughly around the time of Jesus appeared among the documents of the Dead Sea, it was then possible to compare the text of that new document, one which was a thousand years closer to Isaiah than ever before discovered to validate the scholars' belief.

Were the Hebrews as meticulous in preserving their Scriptures as they were reputed to be? Everyone was anxious to see whether a gap of a thousand years would produce significant differences in the contents of the two copies of Isaiah. They discovered that the literary differences between the previous copies of the prophet and the newest treasure were negligible. A thousand years of transmission within the Hebrew community of the prophet's words and deeds produced no significant changes whatever. The Hebrew method of caring for and passing on accurate historical data was vindicated beyond anyone's expectations.

Johns Hopkins professor W. F. Albright spent a lifetime examining the production, accuracy of transmission, and historical reliability of the Old Testament records. He remarks:

> There can be no doubt that archaeology has confirmed the substantial historicity of the Old Testament tradition.[2]

Far from being something the believer needs to apologize for, confidence in the integrity and accuracy of the Bible is entirely warranted by the facts. Regarding both Old and New Testaments, Albright concludes:

> Biblical historical data are accurate to an extent far surpassing the ideas of any modern critical students, who have consistently tended to err on the side of hypercriticism.[3]

No other literature of the ancient world comes to us with such strong credentials.

Moreover, the preservation and transmission of the deeds and words of Jesus are among the most reliable ever to survive the ravages of time. You can count on this: Not a single document or collection of documents from the ancient world can claim a superior – for most, even an equal – standing to that of the New Testament.

"Apart from the Bible, There Is No Historical Evidence for Jesus"

> *"Apart from the New Testament there is no evidence that Jesus ever even existed. Outside this single source there are no other reports of him. Since I don't believe in the Bible, or have any respect for it, this so-called 'evidence' has no effect on me."*

At first hearing, this frequent statement might stop the enthusiastic but inexperienced believer with an "I'll get back to you on that." But there are several things transparently wrong with it, and it can easily be dismissed from the start.

First, the objection by itself makes little sense. Our primary source for the identity of Jesus Christ is the New Testament, mainly the Gospels and parts of the letters of Paul, where early hymns or creeds describing Jesus are preserved. The documents that make up the New Testament are there because they were believed to be the most reliable of all the Gospels and letters that were circulating in the ancient world. The church sorted through the sources that made authoritative claims and decided which should or should not be included in the "Canon," the final, approved collection of accepted documents.

We should always keep in mind that the church never tried to *confer* authority upon the canonical documents, but simply to *confirm* – to recognize or acknowledge – their inherent authority. What happened in the subsequent church councils was not to decide for the first time which documents were worthy of being received, but to ratify what were already widely acknowledged to be the best attested and most reliable writings throughout Christendom.

Think about this parallel. Suppose we were personally responsible for finding and selecting those sources most likely to be reliable accounts of the life and teaching of Jesus. What criteria would we use to sort through the available information about him? If we really were concerned about accuracy, we would want some eye- and ear-witnesses behind the sources. If the apostles, who lived with Jesus day and night for three years, were known to be those closest to him, we would want the name of an apostle to be in some way behind the document. We would want that person to be either the writer of it, or at least standing closely behind it, controlling the information.

This might even include a circle of people around a particular apostle. Also, knowing that secretaries were often used as the actual writers of ancient documents (apparently Paul used them frequently), we would want to make sure that the secretary was close to a firsthand witness.

Then we would want to make sure that the written source was broadly accepted by the greatest possible number of trusted people. Relying upon some small, insignificant sect claiming authority for their source against the testimony of many people in a wide variety of locations would not be a wise choice. The complete family of believers in many places and with many firsthand sources available would be chosen to ensure the greatest degree of accuracy and reliability.

Also, we would want to be certain that the degree of

"historical overlap" was high. If something really happened and wasn't simply the product of an overactive imagination, then we would be most likely to get reliable information from sources that agreed, at least on the essential points.

The following are three of the main criteria which the early church used in order to assemble the basic documents of the New Testament "Canon." They may be referred to as *apostolicity*, *universality*, and *continuity*:

(1) *Apostolicity*. Did an apostle either write or, in some significant way, stand behind the document? In other words, was there an eyewitness available?

(2) *Universality*. What was the extent to which the whole church recognized the document? Put simply, did it pass the sniff test of a great many people who were looking for the truth of the things reported?

(3) *Continuity, Unity, and Consistency*. Was the document in substantial agreement with the other generally accepted sources?

These standards of acceptance are those which could easily come from a modern university history class. They are common sense criteria for determining from a host of claims for authority what should or should not be accepted as reliable. They could be applied to virtually any type of historical document claiming to report something true about a person or a movement.

In addition, to argue that since there is no other evidence for Jesus outside the New Testament, making what we read suspect, is to argue in a circle. Let me use an illustration. Say someone searched far and wide to gather up all the most reliable documents about the life of Napoleon and named the collection the "Napoleonic Canon" (the NC). Only the most authoritative and widely attested of the sources were included. Any document that was considered spurious or created too many questions was excluded.

Then comes the skeptic who wants to study the life of Napoleon and says, "We can't know anything for sure about Napoleon because there is no reliable evidence outside the NC. Show me where else outside the NC I can find the real evidence."

The most natural answer to this would be, "If any other reliable evidence for Napoleon existed, then by definition it would have ended up in the NC. Your objection carries no weight."

Often we hear, "I simply can't accept the evidence from the Bible." A good response to that is, "What part of the Bible don't you accept? Is it Genesis, or Kings, or Isaiah, or some other part? Is it Matthew, Mark, Luke, John, or the letters of Paul? Each was written by a different author, in a different time period, in a different context, and with different reasons. Each has a history of its own with its own particular textual and literary characteristics and problems. Each must be approached as an individual production and evaluated on its own merits."

The objector, who most likely has done little or no historical examination of these documents, may think for another brief moment and say, "I reject the whole Bible." This is probably due to some respected teacher or professor of the past who said to him at one time, "The Bible is just a collection of myths by unlearned ancients," or some such thing. But to reject the entire Bible without even examining the contents, authorship, manuscript verification, reasons for inclusion, and historical background of each document, is like the person who says, "I reject the Napoleonic Canon in its entirety."

Having said all that, there remains one more fact that

renders the initial objection meaningless. The truth is that the New Testament is not the only source of information about Jesus. It's the primary and most reliable collection of sources, but not the only place where bits and pieces of information about him appear in the ancient world. Data about Jesus and the early church is found in the writings of both pagan and hostile Jewish sources.

Some years ago, a professor at a famous university informed me that there was no information about Jesus outside the New Testament. Our short exchange went like this:

> "Yes, there is!"
> "No, there's not!"
> "Yes, there is!"
> "No, there's not!"

After this witty repartee, I decided that there is no substitute for facts. I went to the university library, picked out a book on the sources of Jesus, and presented it to him. It was the classic work in the field, F. F. Bruce's *The New Testament Documents: Are They Reliable?* The book was returned a few weeks later, but not a single word was ever said about the subject again.

The sources containing references to Jesus and the early Christians are as follows:

- Thallus (mid-first century). Book III of his *Histories.*
- Mara Bar-Serapion (late first century). Personal letter.
- Pliny (early second century). *Epistles*, X.96–97.
- Lucian (second century), *DP*, 11–13.
- Tacitus (mid-first century). *Annals*, xiii. 32; xv. 44.
- Suetonius (late first, early second century). *Life of Domitian*, xv. 1; *Dio Cassius*, lxvii. 14; *Life of Nero*, xvi. 2; *Life of Claudius*, xxv. 4.

- Josephus (first century). *Antiquities*, xviii. 3.3.
- Babylonian Talmud, *Sanhedrin*, 43a.

To be sure, such information is scanty and often highly biased against Jesus and the Christians, but it's there for the student to examine and make individual judgments. It appears in exactly that place where it would most likely appear – in the "police records" of ancient Roman society.[4] In its infant stages, the "sect" known as "the Christians" was just an insignificant group in the empire that got its name in the news from time to time for running afoul of the law. It was the function of the early "apologists," or defenders of the church's beliefs (e.g., Ignatius, Justin, Athenagoras, Irenaeus), to persuade the authorities that legal charges against them were of no merit. Then as now, Christians were victims of slander. Even the Roman Emperor Trajan was told that Christians were sexually promiscuous cannibals who loved to start fires!

As minimal as the information about Jesus and the early Christians is in these documents, a core of facts in line with the reports in the New Testament can still be observed. He was known as a miracle worker, he made claims to unusual authority, he caused great disturbances, and he was crucified on a Roman cross.

What is surprising is that there are any references at all to Jesus in the secular documents of the empire. There was no massive church structure to talk about, and there were no famous or powerful people pulling for the relatively insignificant company of believers. The Christians were just not news.

If someone asserts that the Bible is "just another book" that he has no particular respect for and sees no reason to grant it any special considerations, then so be it. Fair enough. At least it's somewhere you can start. The Bible shouldn't be given any free passes or special privileges denied to other literature. It should earn its way into our respect. It stands on its own merits or not at all. If it really is the lion it's said to be, then it doesn't need to be handled like a newborn lamb.

All that's required is that it's given the chance to prove itself. Neither undue reverence for it, nor unwarranted prejudice against it, is a fair place to start. It should be put through all the normal tests and challenges of any other book. Run it through any trial you choose, so long as it's the same as for any other ancient literature. Consider the results for yourself. The evidence is there.

"What About the Other Gospels?"

It's not uncommon to hear reports from the media about other gospels of Jesus in the ancient world which the church has since squelched or is somehow now "covering up." Every year we expect to see the release of yet another book claiming to recover "the real Jesus."

We are continually confronted with the latest Jesus *du jour*. It's very common for some professor of religion somewhere to appear on TV claiming, "There were other gospels around in Jesus' days which the church doesn't like to talk about, but they're just as legitimate as the ones preserved in the New Testament." Often there is a hint of conspiracy in these remarks, creating in the minds of the uninformed the impression that the church has done everything in its power to keep people from discovering these valuable and reliable sources of early Christian history.

Fortunately, the problem is easily solved – reading the so-called "other gospels" for yourself will cure you of your doubts. They range from obviously strange to humorous or grotesque. They are dated late in the game, generations (even one to three centuries) after the eyewitnesses were alive, possessing none of the qualities or credentials of the biblical Gospels which would give them any real historical credibility.

Just so there's no misunderstanding, I'm not referring to the Apocrypha, those books included in the Roman Catholic Bible, for instance. Rather, the "other gospels" refers to those written after the first century in the name of some original apostle of Jesus and which were not included in the Bible.

As well-intentioned as some of them might have been, they were recognized immediately in their time to be nonsense and weren't taken seriously by anyone looking for reliable information about Jesus and the early church. We can compare them to our local supermarket tabloids, relating far-fetched stories of people being abducted by aliens, sightings of long-dead rock stars, and the like.

If you're genuinely concerned about the other gospels, I encourage you to do a personal study of them. One of the most popular is the *Gospel of Thomas*, a mid-second-century concoction designed as a vehicle to advance the philosophy of Gnosticism (opposed by the New Testament). Starting with *Thomas* should cure you of any doubts about the other gospels. It shouldn't take you more than one afternoon of reading to put this whole question to rest.

If you're still curious, I've included some of the typical sayings from the 114 which occur in this "gospel."[5] They come not with any historical context, but as independent sayings loosely strung together. See what you think:

> These are the secret sayings that the living Jesus spoke and Didymos Judas Thomas recorded.
>
> 1. And he said, "Whoever discovers the interpretation of these sayings will not taste death."

4. Jesus said, "The person old in days won't hesitate to ask a little child seven days old about the place of life, and that person will live. For many of the first will be last, and will become a single one."

7. Jesus said, "Lucky is the lion that the human will eat, so that the lion becomes human. And foul is the human that the lion will eat, and the lion still will become human."

11. Jesus said, "This heaven will pass away, and the one above it will pass away. The dead are not alive, and the living will not die. During the days when you ate what is dead, you made it come alive. When you are in the light, what will you do? On the day when you were one, you became two. But when you become two, what will you do?"

14. Jesus said to them, "If you fast, you will bring sin upon yourselves, and if you pray, you will be condemned, and if you give to charity, you will harm your spirits."

15. Jesus said, "When you see one who was not born of woman, fall on your faces and worship. That one is your Father."

22b. Jesus said to them, "When you make the two into one, and when you make the inner like the outer and the outer like the inner, and the upper like the lower, and when you make male and female into a single one, so that the male will not be male nor the female be female, when you make eyes in place of an eye, a hand in place of a hand, a foot in place of a foot, an image in place of an image, then you will enter [the kingdom]."

84. Jesus said, "When you see your likeness, you are happy. But when you see your images that came into being before you and that neither die nor become visible, how much you will have to bear!"

Had enough? Thoroughly confused? I've added a few more pearls of wisdom just to drive home the point.

> 87. Jesus said, "How miserable is the body that depends on a body, and how miserable is the soul that depends on these two."

> 98. Jesus said, "The Father's kingdom is like a person who wanted to kill someone powerful. While still at home he drew his sword and thrust it into the wall to find out whether his hand would go in. Then he killed the powerful one."

> 105. Jesus said, "Whoever knows the father and the mother will be called the child of a whore."

> 112. Jesus said, "Damn the flesh that depends on the soul. Damn the soul that depends on the flesh."

> 114. Simon Peter said to them, "Make Mary leave us, for females don't deserve life." Jesus said, "Look, I will guide her to make her male, so that she too may become a living spirit resembling you males. For every female who makes herself male will enter the kingdom of Heaven."

"The Ancient World Was Full of Dying and Rising Saviors"

In almost any university, the new student of religion will encounter the claim that since the ancient world in which Christianity was born was so filled with "dying and rising savior gods," Jesus must be just another one in the pantheon of popular deities. It is typically argued that since these other "savior gods" existed before Jesus, the New Testament merely borrowed from these stories.

Not much time need be spent on this theory. It evaporates

within a few minutes of cross-examination. First, these "savior gods" were myths constructed out of the imaginations of their creators. They were intended to be understood along the same lines as Greek and Roman mythology (as to the origins and antics of the gods, for example), but it was never suggested that they should be regarded as history.

The New Testament, on the other hand, declares along with the Old Testament that what is described was genuine history – real events in the lives of real people. Since the writers of the Bible were convinced that God had revealed Himself on this earth where His words could be heard and His actions observed, they had little interest in the fables of the pagan world. That's why biblical writers tied their reports to other current events. They weren't imaginary things that happened "once upon a time" in an imagined prehistory, but in specific places at specific times to specific people. Historical study and archeology have consistently vindicated the history within both the Old and New Testaments.

Finally, the "pre-Christian" stories of the dying and rising saviors come down to us from written sources dated long after the time of the New Testament. Common sense would argue that if any borrowing was going on, then the later (the sources of pagan mythology) could easily have borrowed from the earlier (the New Testament). The heavy burden of proof rests upon the objector.

The theory that the early Christians borrowed from these ancient myths to construct their own savior is itself a superstition which has been dying and rising with Draculean regularity since the late 1800s. Although it was laid to rest by the scholars of the 1920s, it still has managed to rise again in each new generation, invariably promoted as a new and stunning revelation about the origins of Christian faith.

Just as in the case of the "other gospels," the best way to dispel your doubts regarding pre-Christian pagan mythology is to read these ancient "fairy tales for adults" yourself. The profound differences are glaring and abundant.[6]

"We Can't Believe Bible Scholars – They're Already Convinced"

The thought that Bible scholars are already convinced and therefore what they tell us can't be trusted, is far from the truth. By and large, those who study the Bible professionally or academically are generally just like those who study Shakespeare or the Greek and Latin classics. Sometimes they are believers in the Bible, either Jewish or Christian, but more often than not, they're simply people interested in the field.

Major universities around the world – such as Harvard, Princeton, Yale, Oxford, Cambridge, and Basel – have biblical studies departments made up of atheists, universalists, Gnostics, believers in every religion under the sun, as well as people who don't care one way or the other. They all represent biases on every side. So when someone writes, "Bible scholars say..." this by itself carries no specific meaning whatever.

Some scholars say one thing, others say another. Biblical scholarship is just as given to fads and fashions as any other field, so what one professor believes will often shift to another theory in the next decade. Popular theories rise and fall with the seasons. In addition, the academic world, supposedly the "marketplace of ideas," has its own orthodoxies which are just as rigid and strongly enforced and come with as many professional penalties as those of any medieval church hierarchy.

You can find Bible scholars anywhere on the spectrum of faith, from devout commitment to radical unbelief. My personal experience is that there are more people among Bible scholars who are not believers than who are. Those who aren't believers often begin their work with the assumption that the supernatural just can't happen, there can't be any miracles, any resurrections, any angels or demons, and so forth. Therefore, if the Bible contains any reports of such things it must be in error and needs some alternative explanation. So it shouldn't surprise us to hear that most scholars "don't agree that the Bible is historically reliable and that Jesus is the only way."

In any case, it's entirely untrue to say that they can't be trusted because they are biased in favor of Jesus and his claims. Many are just as biased against his claims. We should keep in mind that many top scholars who began their research as young, radical skeptics ended their careers as firm believers in Jesus and defenders of the New Testament.

4:
what's the
alternative?

The Counter Challenge

Let's agree for argument's sake that Jesus did make, or at least could have made, the claim that he is the only way to God. Is it still too hard to believe? Does it still seem intolerant and unfair toward the rest of the world with its multiplicity of religions? One way to approach this is to ask what the logical alternatives would be. If Jesus is *not* the only way – if he is merely one way among many – how would that work out in practical terms? What would it look like?

Of course on the surface of things, the idea of many ways to salvation sounds good. It gives an appearance of being open-minded, fair-handed, and just plain up-to-date.

But take a quick look at the logical quagmire this seeming standard of modern thought creates in real, practical terms. To begin with, if we really want to be consistent and above all things to be fair to everyone, then we must insist that each and every religious claim gets its hearing in court. We dare not be selective in this process and accept the religion of one person while excluding that of another. Otherwise, we would become guilty of the very thing we find ourselves accusing others of doing.

We need to bring every religious claim from the north, south, east, and west – to hear from the wisdom of the ancients and the moderns, the simple and the profound. Honesty would demand this. Right now, let's stay totally open to all claims and move forward as broad-minded as we can be.

What Would You Do?

Let's just say that you're any normal, intelligent, and clear-thinking person who wants to make yourself known to a great number of other people. How would you explain yourself to others? Would you disclose yourself in one clear, decisive way without ambiguity? Or would you reveal yourself in one way in one place, and in a completely different or opposite way somewhere else?

In the same way, let's assume that if there is a God out there somewhere, then He most likely would be at least as intelligent and clear thinking as those of us He designed and made. Now, would you expect Him to reveal Himself as an infinite, personal God to one group of people, but as a finite, impersonal force to another? Would He disclose Himself as a God of great love and affection here, and one of absolute non-feeling there? Would He pronounce His disapproval of hatred and violence in one location, but His love for it – and even requirement of it – elsewhere?

What about His laws, His rules, His preferences? Would He require moral and sexual purity of one group, but be absolutely indifferent to it, or even allow unbounded self-indulgence, in another? Would He proclaim His hatred and prohibition of revenge to one part of the earth's population, and yet demand it of another?

Such questions could be multiplied all day long. If we believe that every religion is a way to God or ultimate salvation, then these are the questions we must face. For each "way" portrays God (if God is even believed in at all) in a radically different manner, despite our local professor of religion who decrees that all religions are more or less the same, or are trying to get at the same thing in different ways.

What Are the Facts?

The plain facts are these: One sincere set of followers thinks that God is pleased when hatred is directed toward those outside the group. Another feels that God is pleased when love is expressed to those of another belief system. One deeply devoted person honestly and strongly believes that God is honored by the violent death of the unbeliever, but the other is equally convinced that God is honored by love and mercy extended to the unbeliever. Each is one hundred percent sure that God is the source of their belief. Then there's the group who is convinced that there is no such personal God capable of revealing His will to human beings in the first place.

We can trace the same inconsistencies as we probe deeper into the cores of each faith system. The same kinds of differences appear. To one faithful believer, ultimate salvation comes about by doing works of the law, keeping the rules, performing the rites, fulfilling the requirements of the religion. Another teaches exactly the opposite – salvation comes by trust in God alone and in what this God has done for the believer. For this person salvation can't be earned under any circumstances whatever by good works or fulfillment of any rule or law.

Let's move farther on and in. One group thinks that we are saved from sin. Another, that we are saved from the false belief that there is such a thing as sin. One religion sees future salvation as a redemption and renewal of the physical world. Another sees it as the annihilation of the physical world. One hopes for the survival of the human personality and reunion of friends and loved ones. Another is equally convinced that all personality and consciousness will be absorbed and disappear altogether for eternity into a great universal "oneness."

There's more. One values kindness, mercy, and compassion. Another values the correct performance of religious rites and rituals. Yet another values cruelty toward those who disagree with the religion. One holds in high esteem the convinced worshipper. Another esteems the one who does not belong to the faith. One places a high valuation on the physical world and its conditions for life. Another thinks that the physical world is either an illusion or irrelevant. One considers history as critically important and meaningful. Another, that history is without meaning or purpose.

Don't forget! We agreed at the beginning that one person's religious claims are just as good as another's. Therefore, we must agree on the one hand that what the Christian claims is legitimate – namely, that salvation comes by humbly accepting the free gift brought about by the work of Christ on the cross alone, apart from works of self-effort. On the other hand, we must also accept the view that salvation and the reward of paradise are gained by murdering innocent men, women, and children in the most cruel ways possible. We must admit the claim that our personal salvation comes through ridding the world of those we disagree with and love to hate.

Making the Point Even Clearer

Thus far, our desire to admit every belief system into the court of acceptability leads us to the point of opening our arms to everyone's beliefs and practices. What happens when we make this concession? Let's take an even closer and longer look.

The rules and rites of some religions have required some very odd or frightening things. Let's glance back at the ancient world.

A Canaanite worshipper walks solemnly toward the massive bronze figure with their greatest treasure in hand – their child. At the prescribed moment, the worshipper tosses the child into the red-hot iron bowl formed by the hands of the idol. Priests nearby pound wildly on the drums to drown out the screams of pain. The heat is so intense, the small body almost explodes on contact. The god is pleased with the sacrifice. It will be a good year for the people.

In the dead of night, a man steals onto the steps of the Roman Forum to pick up a baby left there by an unwilling parent. If a boy, it's taken to be trained for a lifetime of slavery. If a girl, she's taken immediately to the temple where she is raised and trained at a very early age to be of service to the many men who come to "worship" through the act of temple prostitution.

A priest of a second-century AD mystery religion stands before the pit on which a live bull has been fastened on a grating above. He climbs down into the pit just as the bull is slit open by a large knife, allowing the hot blood to flow over him. He lets the red wave flow over his head and beard, into his eyes and ears, and even opens his mouth in order to let it cover him both inside and out. By this ritual, he hopes to rid himself of humanity's universal sense of stain in need of cleansing and thinks himself to be spiritually purified and regenerated. With total religious devotion, he comes to perform his prescribed worship at the *Taurobolium*.

Here is a dark example from Arabia which occurred in March AD 626. In an unprovoked attack upon their fortress, about 2,000 Jewish people of Beni Koreiza were taken by force, and 800 men were separated from their families. The wives and children were set apart and kept out of sight, while the men were detained in a separate camp. All waited through the day and far into the next night, assuming that the small groups of five or six men, who were being called out from the great crowd every few moments and led away, were just being questioned or processed for relocation.

The first light of day revealed the full horror. Numerous large trenches had been dug in the middle of the town market place. Each small group of Jewish men was led to the brink and made to sit down, then one by one all 800 were beheaded and tossed into the trenches. It took the entire day and part of the night to complete. The women and children were kept as slaves for life. All this was done at the order of a religious "prophet" who believed that this sincere act of pious devotion would be to his eternal credit and to the great glory of God.

Take a familiar scene from the medieval period: A priest stands by giving orders to the sweaty, muscular men operating the rack. He watches as the victim is stretched over the huge device and tied down. He listens as the crank is turned, causing the sinews and tendons of the person's body to snap and tear loose. He is unmoved by the victim's screams because, in his mind, this is what God decrees for those who disagree with the statements of the church hierarchy. He takes comfort in what he has been taught by religious leaders gone astray – that he is doing the work of his Lord. He is wholly unaware that Jesus taught the exact opposite.

One religion which our openness must take seriously demands the torture and mutilation of those of other tribes and religions, culminating in the tearing off or out of the body various body parts and eating them in front of the stunned victim. A type of salvation flows from the act of cruel sacrifice of the poor, unsuspecting prey. In some cases, the greater the cruelty on the part of the torturer and the greater pain on the part of the tortured, the greater the reward for the former. Such was the fate of a sixteenth-century French priest who entered the forests of what is now known as New England in hopes of bringing the Christian Gospel to the Indian inhabitants.

Here's another example. The word thug in English usually refers to a cutthroat, gangster, ruffian, or mugger. But originally it referred to a sect of religious fanatical assassins. Induction was passed from father to son. In Asia, these bands of roving criminals tracked, sometimes for weeks, and wormed themselves into the confidence of their victims (particularly wealthy ones) then murdered and robbed them.

These brutal assassins didn't care how young their victims were. Killing was accomplished by joining a group of travellers and entertaining and cooking for them. Taking them off guard by lulling them into a false sense of security, the victims were strangled and goods plundered. The murders were conducted according to precise, rigid religious rites to honor their goddess, Death – it was her will. Each murder appeased her and prevented her arrival for 1000 years.

Some rituals which go back into the distant past are still practiced in some regions of the world. *Sati*, for example, is seen as a highly venerable act of a virtuous woman who allows herself to be burned alive on the funeral pyre with her dead husband. In spite of the Sati Prevention Act in India, certain sects still consider it as the way a woman redeems her deceased ancestors who may be rotting in hell and assures her entrance straight into heaven. Some see such a sacrifice as granting great benefits to the family for up to seven generations. Even though, theoretically, it is entirely voluntary on the part of the widow, due to these great benefits, family members often make sure that the woman does her filial duty whether she wants to or not.

In some countries, there is still a high regard for – even worship of – the rats of the city. They are treated so well that while they grow fat with grain from the offerings, the children living on nearby streets starve for lack of food.

In parts of the world today there still thrives the same ancestor terrorism that for centuries has trapped great numbers of people in profound fear and dread. They live in constant anxiety that their ancestors will be so displeased that as a consequence a curse will be placed upon them. Avoiding these curses becomes the principal motivation behind much of their behavior. An elaborate (and expensive) system of worship has developed to protect the living from all kinds of evils thought to come from dead relatives.

When a child falls sick, for example, one of the best animals is sacrificed to please the ancestor, thus affecting the family economy. When someone in the extended family dies, a costly funeral is required to prevent ancestor recrimination, thus further devastating the family's financial welfare. With AIDS rampant and funerals frequent, ongoing poverty is guaranteed for all. At the center of this superstition-riddled faith is the local witch doctor who, for high fees, is willing to identify the one responsible for a curse. For even more money, he offers his services to place a counter-curse upon the guilty party (if living), or to prescribe some remedy to placate an angry ancestor. Many of these "professionals" even serve as key advisors to local and national politicians, thus shaping the country's domestic and foreign policies.[1]

For some, ancestor worship takes the form of young women being called upon by the community to perform simulated sex acts with a drum, believed to be the point of contact with the ancestral gods. While drums beat vigorously, the virtually naked woman works herself into a drug induced state of frenzy to carry out this rite before the other worshippers. The highest pitched drum is dedicated to the gods, so that her performance with it, if accepted, hopefully will result in the peace and prosperity of the village. Ancestor worship is often associated with sexuality, including ritual sex acts between humans and animals.

Consider a few more examples. On January 23, 1999, a missionary and his two sons were dragged from their car in the remote village of Manoharpur in India, mercilessly beaten, then shoved back into their vehicle and prevented from escaping while it was set on fire. People who tried to help the victims were stopped by the killers. This was a sacred act by highly religious people who hated those of another religion, a type of sacrament performed by those devoted to their faith.

On September 11, 2001, the Twin Towers of the World Trade Center in New York City were turned into towering infernos incinerating several thousand people trapped helplessly inside. The intent was to kill the potential 50,000 or so workers who ordinarily would be there by midmorning on any typical work day. This act was done by religious militants who believed that killing as many "infidels" as possible was a very good thing, thoroughly approved – even required – by God.

These devoted *mujahids* operated from a double motivation. On the one hand, they were convinced that they were propelling themselves into paradise. On the other, they believed that they were sending their victims not only to their deaths, but to eternal torment. This was a religious work, pure and simple. Whatever geopolitical overtones it might have had were incidental. The religious explanation was clearly given by the planners and perpetrators themselves.

On Sunday, October 28, 2001, three gunmen entered a Christian church in Bahawalpur, Pakistan and machine-gunned down several hundred worshippers. Men, women, and children lay in pools of blood around the sanctuary. Again, the killers were doing their duty, shouting, "God is Great" and, "Graveyard of Christians – Pakistan and Afghanistan," before opening fire. They were doing the very "work of God."

Of course many, if not most, people within the world's religions are peace loving. The point of all the above is not that all the religions are violent, but that virtually all violence is part of someone's religion. Whatever base, vile, or unimaginably ruthless behavior that has occurred in some part of the world at some period in history; whatever form of butchery, rape, cannibalism, suicide, self-mutilation, pedophilia, drunkenness or abuse that can be observed; whatever hatred, revenge, crusade, immorality, debauchery, or atrocity that can be considered, often turns out to be an ingredient of someone's sincerely held belief system somewhere.

Space and time do not permit a full description of all the human sacrifice, sexual perversion, blood or urine drinking, torture, revenge, tongue-slicing, pain-inflicting, drug-taking acts of devotion that make up the world of religion. The textbooks are replete with such illustrations.

Obviously then, the great danger of leveling all religions is that it totally undercuts the possibility of distinguishing good from evil. The lines become hopelessly blurred. If my neighbor's religion commands him to murder me in the most barbaric way he can think of, or to commit genocide, then what becomes of the differences between good and evil? If everyone's religion or religious expression, no matter what it is, is good and right, then there's nothing left to the meaning of the word "good." There is no evil left to judge, for it has been taken up into the arms of "religion." It has been said that religion is a dangerous thing unless we get it right! If we fail to get it right, then we'll be led straight back to the law of the jungle.[2]

Let me say in passing that a strange irony emerges as we think further along these lines. The presence in the world of the evils mentioned above is frequently used to argue that there is no God, or that if there is one, He must be either indifferent or blatantly cruel. How many times have we heard the question (or even thought ourselves), "How could a loving God allow such suffering and injustice in the world?" Yet if we try to argue that all religions are pathways to God and salvation, we end up affirming that such evils are not only allowed but actually *required* by God!

On the one hand, then, we would hear the protest, "How could a just God allow such things?" On the other, we would hear, "How could a just God *not* allow such things, so long as they were performed in the name of some religion?" But what kind of deity would the latter be? The view of Russian atheist Mikhail Bakunin would then make more sense: If God existed, He would have to be destroyed.

Keep in mind, we dare not recoil at, turn away from, or prefer any religion without violating the first principle of "openness to diversity" we began with. We can't choose only those religions we like or approve. We must either admit all religions or none. We can't approach them with some preconceived standard by which to measure them and still be faithful to our original commitment to avoid "bigotry" and remain "tolerant."

Neither can we get away with saying that people who do "bad" things aren't the real representatives of those religions, but rather only those who do good, kind, and nice things. Who are we to say that their good, kind, and nice things are the standard for others to live up to? How do we know who the real representatives of any religion are? How do we find out? Do we ask them?

Remember, we mustn't try to evaluate sincere worshippers from the perspective of our own culture or religious experience. This is exactly what we agreed earlier should not happen if we are to remain accepting of all sincere religious expression. As we are told repeatedly, "We can't apply our own beliefs or preferences as absolute standards for others."

It should become obvious, without belaboring the point any further, that the more religions we study, the more varied, creative, and even shocking are the ways "salvation" is thought to be achieved. In fact, the most common characteristic of the world's religions is this: It is *something achieved*. It is the product of one's own efforts. In whatever distorted or twisted form, the method remains the same. It's believed to come from the work and efforts of the devotee, or not at all.

This is the expressed antithesis of the Christian faith which claims, on the authority of Jesus Christ, that salvation comes to us as a free gift – totally unearned and unearnable, granted by the sheer mercy and grace of the God who created us. It's a finished work accomplished by the death of Jesus on the cross and cannot be improved upon or embellished by our efforts. It's not in any way achieved. It is freely and humbly received as a child accepts a gift, or it is not received at all.

Many Ways to What?

Before we leave this area, we should spend a few more minutes thinking about what we are often told has many ways leading to it – salvation. If there really are many ways and not just one clear, definitive way, then what is the destination of these many ways? What exactly is the salvation we imagine we are striving for?

What is surprising to many who pursue these questions is the fact that there really are very few options available in the world religion supermarket. If we survey the variety of ideas offered us, we arrive at just a handful of pictures of what our eternal destiny looks like. If we dismiss the idea of "nothing-ness" (annihilation), which hardly qualifies as a form of salva-tion, then we're left with just two life-after-death options to choose from. Everything else on the market is merely a varia-tion or "heresy" of them.

On the one hand, we have the view from Eastern thought which affirms that we are locked into a system of soul migrations or repeated incarnations (birth, death, rebirth, and so forth) until we reach the end of this cycle. We are finally absorbed into what is barely distinguishable from what we usually recognize as annihilation. This view sees the physical world as purely temporary or illusory. Only the spirit or the nonphysical is of any real importance. The body, the earth, the universe, and all that there is will one day simply not exist.[3]

Biblical Salvation

The other basic model comes to us from the Judeo-Christian tradition. We'll look at this in some detail because it's common for both Christians and non-Christians alike to be very fuzzy on what it is that Jesus offers as the "only way." Not only is the picture of final destiny different from what other faiths teach, it's also different from what most Christians imagine the Bible teaches on the subject.

This model is referred to in the New Testament as God's "purpose" or "plan" (Ephesians 1:11–14; Acts 2:22–24). This plan is what we should expect from a purposeful and rea-sonable God. The universe with all its planets, moons, and stars seems very much a matter of order and design, whether viewed from China, Switzerland, or South Africa. Forces which govern them appear fixed and unyielding.

Why would the Creator of all things do less planning and be less organized than any fire department or ball team? Intelligent beings plan what is important to them, and the more important something is, the more planning goes into it. Anything less than a clear strategy of salvation for God's highest creatures would be very odd indeed.

There are two ways of discovering a city's bus plan. We can jump on any bus thinking we know where it's going and hope for the best, or we can learn the bus plan and board the one going where we want to go. I've tried both approaches and strongly recommend the second!

The plan, as outlined in the New Testament, affirms first that there is a God who is very personal, who created us in His image, and that we are fallen from our high position as the crown of His creation. It states that our real problem is "sin," which is what separates us from this holy God and can be resolved only by the merciful act of our Creator and it spells out very clearly that He brings us home by a great sovereign work of rescue. It cannot in any way depend upon our own works or effort. Ultimate human destiny will be life either in a physical, resurrected body on a physical, renewed earth, or in final destruction, eternal separation from God and all that is good.

The idea that the spirit will one day be separated from the physical body and physical realm and dwell forever in a heaven of pure spirit is not a Hebrew or a Christian idea. Rather, it comes from ancient, pagan philosophy. The fact that many, if not most, Christians today hold to this view in some way proves how thoroughly alien pagan belief systems have permeated the church.

Christians often miss the point on another level. They believe that ultimate salvation is far beyond our ability even to imagine and are fond of citing the passage in 1 Corinthians 2:9 in support of this view:

As it is written: 'No eye has seen, no ear has heard, no mind has conceived what God has prepared for those who love him.'

However, Paul's whole point in this passage (read it again in context) is not that believers are unable to imagine what our eternal destiny is like, but that what earlier generations could not possibly imagine *can* now be seen clearly in Jesus Christ. What was hidden in the past has now been revealed – we can now see what we could not see before. If there is any conclusion to be drawn from Paul's statement regarding life after death for the believer, then it would have to be that it can and must be imagined. We are encouraged to try to picture it on the basis of what we can know now in the life, death, and resurrection of the Son of God. This is the plan.

What we are to imagine regarding our future destiny is based upon whatever good we can think of in the here and now. What makes up the very best of earthly life? We can recall the very best vacation, the highest love of our lives, the finest dinner ever eaten, the greatest athletic or educational achievement, the most exciting adventure, or the most exhilarating run through the mountains or swim in the surf.

Salvation, as depicted both in the Old and New Testaments, is an earthly, physical existence which involves not only the spirit, but the physical human body, transformed by resurrection, able to do at least what it can do now, but somehow far more. It implies not white, gauzy, ghostlike existence (spirits without bodies), but rather air, water, trees, flowers, sky, lakes and seas, birds and animals, muscles, exercise, sport, work, learning, love, reunion with family and friends, delicious food, and all the rest that makes up our real existence now. At least this is the direction our imaginations should take us.

The principal difference is that evil will be forever gone.

There will be life without death, sickness, aging, pain, suffering, malice, hatred, greed, confusion about God, and the like. It will be where only good dwells. We will live the way we were originally intended to live – a way lost in the Fall of man but restored in the life and work of Jesus, the Son of God. All other faith systems which include some form of personal survival and ongoing existence of the individual human personality borrowed in some way from this biblical model.

These are the choices when looking at some form of ultimate destiny or "salvation." We have before us either traditional Eastern thought or some variant of it, or Judeo-Christianity or some variant of it. True, some of the variations of these have developed over the centuries into systems of earthly ethics with no concern whatever for survival beyond death, so the word "salvation" does not really apply. For some of the spinoff religions of the world, the word "God" or "gods" is now wholly irrelevant and even offensive.

Some Conclusions

What can we conclude so far? When the "all-religions-are-the-same" view is accepted, some very odd consequences follow. Keeping in mind the diversity of the religion market, we face some real intellectual problems if we assert that they all give us accurate but different portraits of life, death, and human destiny. We are left with some enormous obstacles to talking about God at all. Remember, we are not dealing merely with those examples of religious violence, but with religion in general.

We may sum up several of the problems already suggested. When we venture into one region, God is portrayed as one who loves kindness and charity toward our enemies. But when we cross over the border into another country just an hour later, the situation is totally different. When "God" pops up in the religion here, He is one who hates some people and is pleased with the cruel murder of them at the hands of others. God demands performance of works for salvation on one side of the lake, but over on the other side He completely rejects any form of works for salvation.

He is personal in His appearance to one group of people, but totally impersonal (a force or "it") to another. He demands moral holiness and purity for some, but is indifferent to the greatest debauchery for others. On the one hand, He requires the giving of food and shelter to the needy, but on the other is unmoved by the routine death of children so long as grain is supplied to the "holy" rats in the rat temples. Literally hundreds of such moral problems and contradictions may be easily brought forward.

"God" becomes to the universalist a being who has no real personality or consistent character at all. He, she, or it is both good and evil, passionate about justice and indifferent to it at the same time. This God appears in one disguise or mask in one place of the world, and in a totally different disguise in another. If analyzed as we analyze human beings, such a "God" would be considered severely disordered. How could any person who behaves in such a diverse, disintegrated, contradictory, and entirely unpredictable manner be taken seriously? If there is one God behind all the religions of the world, then this God must be diagnosed as demented. If such a being existed, who would want anything to do with Him/Her/It?

So it begins to appear that "many ways to the one God" ultimately leads to the many ways to the many gods. "One and only one way" implies monotheism. "Many ways" or "all ways" implies polytheism. This conclusion seems to be inescapable in light of the great variation in the manifestations of the so-called "many ways." No single, unified Being ("God") could possibly accommodate the extreme diversity of the various "divine" manifestations required by tossing all belief systems into the ring.

Things become even more complicated if we include not only the formal "religious systems," but those other philosophical belief systems which could be classified as "virtual religions," such as Communism or Naziism. These could be regarded as the religions of atheism.

We may confidently discard the view that, whereas there may be a few incidental differences in the externals of each faith, there is nevertheless a common core which makes all faiths pretty much the same. A thorough study of all the world's faiths reveals exactly the opposite. There may be, in fact, a few superficial, external similarities between all faiths (holy books, religious rites to be performed, priests, systems of ethics to follow, and the like), but when you get to the core of each, there are radical differences which cannot be combined into one mix. The differences of world view, answers they give to life's problems, values they hold, ways of salvation, even what "salvation" means, are incapable of being stirred together into one big soup.

If a similar question were raised in any other area of thought, it would seem quite silly. What if someone were to claim boldly that all economic theories are essentially the same, or that all philosophies, political views, or even mathematical equations were more or less the same? Such a statement made in the university would draw great ridicule from others. But when someone makes this kind of suggestion about the world's faiths, it's thought to be the height of reason and good sense. Only someone who has taken the time and effort to study them knows how far afield the claim really is.

In response to that cliché of modern mythology, "All religions are essentially the same," we may cite the remarks of Massachusetts Institute of Technology professor Huston Smith. He has learned more about the religions of the world than most of us and has been widely recognized in academic circles as the dean of world religions. He states:

> A great historian of religion devoted forty years of his life to determining what the world's great religions have in common and came up with two things: "Belief in God – if there be a God" and "Life is worth living – sometimes."[4]

In reality, the only way in which all religions could be "equal" would be if they were *equally worthless,* for we would be in dire need of none of them. Any way we could picture God would be as good, real, or effectual as any other, and it would not matter in the slightest which one we chose since they all led to the same end. If having looked over all the options on the religion menu we still did not like any of the available choices, we could simply create another out of our own imagination. One more religion would make no difference. Whatever flight of fancy we could concoct would be just as good and effectual in reaching salvation as any already on the market.

Many Ways to the One Way

If the phrase "many ways" could be useful at all, it could be said rightly that whereas there are not many ways to God and salvation, there are many ways to the one way. Christian history has demonstrated this millions of times since the first century. People have journeyed wearily across the barren wilderness of false religions, dead-end philosophies, and homemade belief systems, only to be led by the great sovereign hand of the Creator into the knowledge of His only Son.

Great masses of honest seekers in each generation have traveled through one religion after another in search of reality and truth only to find that shadows and gloom met them there. Yet when they first heard clearly the word of life in Jesus Christ, they recognized that this was the one true light compared to which every other system could be described as nothing but "darkness and despair."

No two stories are exactly alike as to how each one of us comes to the knowledge of the eternal Son of God. Every story is a separate and unique pathway to the one true way. We may come to the entryway from a billion different pathways, turning this way and that, but if it's truth we really desire, we eventually arrive at the one door leading into the presence of the one God. In Jesus and Jesus alone God says to us, "I want to make myself known to you in an absolutely clear and unmistakable way so that you can't possibly misunderstand who I am and what I'm like. I am this way and no other!"

Jesus did not come to add to the confusion or profusion of religions, but to dispel and put an end to both. If there is a real, caring, personal God to reckon with, why would He have done it any other way?

The Nature of Faith in Jesus

Coming to real faith in Jesus Christ is never portrayed as just another change from one intellectual position to another. Rather, it's more like emerging from a long fever into the bright morning of health and recovery. It's often described by new converts as coming out from the darkness into the light, from death to life, from confusion to clarity.

Some Christians are so absolutely, positively sure of their faith in Jesus Christ that they actually annoy others because of it. Have you met some of these people? They display no basic or lasting doubts about their faith and to many appear too dogmatic and overly confident to be "real." Of course, we don't doubt that there are some people in the church who have reached their seemingly unshakable certainty by the wrong means. They may be certain just because they may be the kind of persons (we all know them) who think they can't be wrong about anything. If they happen to be Christians, they must be right simply because they are never wrong. But this is not the kind of unshakable faith being described here. Stubborn dogmatism and humble faith are not the same thing.

When the New Testament uses the word "faith," it means something quite different from the way we use it in most of our conversations. By the time the New Testament was translated into the English language, the word chosen to represent the Greek word *pistis* carried with it the same meaning intended by the biblical writers: something rock-solid sure, beyond dispute – a position of certainty at least as strong as the word "knowledge." In fact, biblical faith is something which is based upon knowledge of fact and is considered an *advanced form of knowledge.*

Therefore, when a believer in the ancient world said something like, "I believe that God exists," or, "I believe that Jesus Christ is the risen Son of God and Savior of the world," what they meant was that they were so sure in this confession that if it wasn't true, nothing else was. The believer was prepared to stake both earthly life and eternal destiny on it. It was the foundation of all other knowledge they possessed.

When the early Christians were commanded by the authorities to renounce their faith and were threatened with torture and death of the most grisly kinds, they responded with this surprising and cheerful level of certainty. They were so sure of their standing that it stunned their persecutors. It was this new quality of confidence and assurance that impressed the pagan world and eventually contributed to the overthrow of all its many false gods and religions.

When believers today say, "Jesus is the only way to God," they are not just blindly refusing to consider all the other options on the religion market (a great many of them know the religions of the world well). Rather, they are professing what has been divinely revealed to them in a wide variety of unique and tailor-made ways. Many are stating what they know to be true, whether or not anyone else around them accepts the fact. From their point of view, they are declaring not just a feeling inside them, but a fundamental fact of reality, just as surely as if they were stating a chemical formula or established geometric theorem.

The Gospels and Acts record various incidents where people came to believe in Jesus as each was given a very personal, particular disclosure of Jesus' person and work. The promiscuous woman at the well (John 4:26), the blind man (John 9:1–38), the doubter (John 20:24–28), the Ethiopian government official (Acts 8:26–38), the Philippian jailer (Acts 16:16–34), and many more were granted just the right evidence at the right moment to persuade them that what the Gospel claimed was true. The personality, individual quirks, loves, hates and fears, education, and intelligence level of each was taken into consideration by God in His mysterious providence in bringing a wide variety of people to unwavering faith. This has been true for the last 2,000 years of church history.

Such is the nature of faith in Jesus Christ. However, this quality of surety doesn't come merely by study or contemplation, although they play a role in its development. This startling confidence comes by means which God alone engineers and imparts. It is the result usually of a prolonged season of maturation – evergrowing enlightenment, study of fact, and confirmation by life experience. The definition of faith used in this book is: *Faith is informed trust based on fact and confirmed by experience.* It is a relationship with God founded on the work of Jesus, established with us by the sheer mercy of God, and imparted through the Holy Spirit.

Faith in Jesus – the kind described in the New Testament – comes to us as a gift from God. It is God who first draws us, prepares us, educates us, demonstrates Himself to us, and continues to prove His existence and faithfulness by preserving us through all of life's ups and downs. Jesus is always a present reality to each generation. The whole point of the Book of Acts, for example, is that since Jesus was raised from death, he is forever alive and present with his church.

But real faith is no good luck charm or magic. It involves a relationship with God and, like any relationship, is subject to variations on our part of feeling and mood. From the human perspective, faith is often like the tides of the sea. One day it appears to go out unexpectedly and then returns again. This in-and-out, up-and-down nature of faith suggests that its Source stands outside us (it's always a gift from the hand of God) and illustrates the fact that what lies beneath and behind it is something more basic, namely, the grace and sustaining power of God. It is God who initially grants faith as a gift, who allows it to ebb and flow for purposes known only to Himself, who sustains it over time, and who recreates it when it has seemingly vanished.

Therefore, we are eternally safe in Jesus Christ not because we possess, or can of our own will produce, enough faith. Rather, we are given the gift of faith because God's mercy upholds us and supplies us with all that we need. Also, the believer isn't someone who lives in a bubble and never has any doubts, but someone whose doubts and crises energize and propel them to seek further knowledge. Faith feeds on fact. It grows and thrives in the soil of reality and truth.

Moreover, we cannot "prove" to someone else in any final

sense the existence or reality of God or Jesus merely with human arguments, but that does not mean that it cannot be proven. This activity is one which God reserves for Himself. God is perfectly able to prove His own existence. He and He alone constructs for us a great variety of personally tailored demonstrations to convince us in ways which far exceed our weak and simple efforts. We come to a confidence in our final resurrection at the end of history based largely upon all the little resurrections or rescues we experience in this life. Whereas we say to Jesus, "Prove to me and I will follow," Jesus says to us, "Follow and I will prove to you." The final proof is in the living of it.

Thus, this level of reality and surety can't really be understood fully by those outside this experience. But as the light brightens for each of us, we come to grasp just why it is that those who at first seemed to us so dogmatic and unyielding are, after all, merely thinking and doing exactly as truth and reality would dictate.

Because of the very specific nature of Christian faith, the New Testament would never use the word "faith" in reference to other religions. All other belief systems would be considered counterfeit. Trust in these systems would be categorized not as another form of faith, but as some form of delusion or superstition. Faith is so interconnected with fact and truth that it would never be used in reference to anything considered false.

The true Christian believes that Jesus is the Christ, the Son of God, the only Savior of the world, not because they are unable to imagine any other religious or philosophical options, but because both the evidence of history and the evidence in their present relationship with God confirm it over and over again.

The idea that Jesus is the only way to God and the only hope of salvation doesn't originate in the mind or personal faith of the believer, but in the declaration of Jesus and his Father. There is an enormous difference between a football fan saying, "My team is the one and only team," and a king saying, "I am decreeing that there is one, and only one, doorway into my kingdom."

The Bible has various ways of describing the experience of coming to sure confidence in God. The Hebrew Psalmist expressed it this way: "Taste and see that the Lord is good" (Psalm 34:8), or in Luther's words, "Taste and see how kind/ friendly (*freundlich*) the Lord is." The New Testament says the same thing in various ways. "Come and see" is the invitation of Jesus, not, "Here's the doctrine – take it or leave it." The Bible always leaves the doubter or skeptic to come and see if it's really true and invites the outsider to come, see, and evaluate the truth of it from the inside. There is never even the slightest mention of "blind faith." Jesus' ever-consistent invitation is: "Come along after me and I will show you. If you will just show up, stay around, and pay attention, I will make it clear to you." Those who do come, even with great hesitation, will in time be convinced of the truth of it.

5:
common questions

Now let's consider the usual questions about the Christian faith as they occur in conversations. Not every question concerns every one of us, but every answer should deepen our understanding of the issue at hand.

(1) What about the people who were not raised in a Christian culture?

Even though this exact question is not directly addressed in the New Testament, there are some facts which give us good reason to have confidence in the justice and fairness of God. In the very beginning of the first Gospel in the New Testament, the Gospel of Matthew, we find the fascinating story of the Magi. While we don't know for sure who these men were, they are famous because of the Christmas hymn *We Three Kings*. But we have no reason to think that they were actually kings or that there were only three; Matthew doesn't tell us.

The scholar's best guess is that they were Babylonian astrologers, the ancient version of astronomers or, in their own right, scientists. They had witnessed a change in the stars which they believed predicted an event of great significance. Following the movement of the new light in the heavens (the star), they arrived at the place where Jesus was born. How much they knew and how they came to know is unclear, but they worshipped the newborn baby.

We do not know why God chose these men to be among the small handful of people to come to the "manger," but they did represent the Gentile world, that mass of the world's population whom many of the traditional religious leaders had written off as unworthy of divine attention. The Gospel writer Luke tells us that in the prophecy of Jesus' birth it was clearly stated that he came as "a light to the Gentiles" (Luke 2:32).

The Magi had their own religious beliefs about the world and what was beyond, but they were led in an entirely unpredictable way to the "one way." From within their own context, God managed in some mysterious manner to communicate the necessity of coming to His Son. They responded to the light they had and were given more.

In the Gospel of John we are clearly told:

> This is the verdict: Light has come into the world, but men loved darkness instead of light because their deeds were evil. Everyone who does evil hates the light, and will not come into the light for fear that his deeds will be exposed.
>
> John 3:19–20

In other words, the object of God's judgment is not so much ignorance of the truth, but the conscious, willful desire to avoid the truth. What attracts God's judgment is the extent to which people prefer darkness to light. Moreover, John adds to our understanding of *epistemology* (a philosophy of knowledge). If the question is asked, "How does one come to a knowledge of truth?" the answer of Jesus is:

> If anyone chooses to do God's will, he will find out whether my teaching comes from God or whether I speak on my own.
>
> John 7:17

Thus far, we may be assured that God calls His people from all parts of the globe to hear the word of Jesus in ways we could never predict.

Let's look at a few more examples from early church history as recorded in Luke's work *The Acts of the Apostles*. In Acts, he introduces us to a series of people known as "God-worshippers." These persons were not officially part of the Jewish or Jewish-Christian faith, but were nevertheless being brought by God into ever-brighter light. Earlier we met the Ethiopian eunuch, an official of his country, whom God caused to cross paths during his travels with Jesus' disciple Philip. From first to last, we are to understand this as a divinely engineered encounter in order to draw the stranger into the kingdom of God.

Later in Acts, we are introduced to other people along the way who loved the truth and were being called into the new faith by God's sovereign design. A centurion is brought to faith in Jesus (10:1–48). Lydia, the businesswoman from the city of Thyatira, meets Paul and his entourage in Philippi. Her home becomes the place where the first church in the history of Europe is planted (16:13–15). Sometime later, a man named Titius Justus, a worshipper of God, is similarly brought to faith (18:7).

We meet an interesting character toward the end of Acts when Paul is shipwrecked on the island of Malta (27:27–28:10). Luke wants us to know that the incident was all part of God's purpose and plan to present the healing and saving news of Jesus to the leading official of the island, as well as to his people. God had prearranged to have Paul make this "stop" on his journey to Rome.

At the end of Luke's Gospel another account is given of a criminal who comes to faith in the last few hours of his life. He is one of two men receiving capital punishment for crimes committed against the empire. What they did exactly, we aren't sure. We know only that they were crucified on either side of Jesus. One of them joined in the mockery of Jesus as he was dying. The second criminal rebuked the first and said that they justly deserved their punishment, but Jesus was innocent of all guilt. He turned to Jesus and said merely, "Jesus, remember me when you come into your kingdom" (23:42).

In this, Jesus perceived a repentant heart and accepted his statement as a full confession, as complete as any that has ever been made. The Psalmist David or Reformer Martin Luther could not have made a more thorough confession of sin and sorrow for it. In these few words, Jesus saw through to his heart of hearts and uttered the words which have echoed down the halls of history, "Today you will be with me in paradise." In one moment of time, the man had moved from darkness to light, from death to life, from total alienation from God to complete and unqualified acceptance in the divine presence. Jesus was faithful to the promise made earlier in his ministry, "All that the Father gives me will come to me, and whoever comes to me I will never drive away" (John 6:37).

If you spend even a few afternoons reading through the biographies of missionaries, you can see beyond a shadow of a doubt that God has an eye on people of every land, language, and culture. Tens of thousands of stories are available which clearly indicate that people of every conceivable belief system even in the most remote regions of the globe are drawn in mysterious ways to Jesus the Son. Sometimes these people are attracted to the light through the missionaries themselves and sometimes through no human agency whatsoever.

So it appears that while there are virtually innumerable pathways which lead to Jesus, there is only one that leads away from him – a preference for darkness and an avoidance of the light. Only the love of our sin will keep us from him.

(2) What about those who never had the chance to hear the name of Jesus?

Once again, this question is not specifically addressed in the New Testament, but we can piece together some facts to give an informed response.

First, we are given basic principles to work with from the very first book of the Bible and throughout both Testaments. In Genesis, the patriarch Abraham faces some challenges he can't easily reconcile with God's promises. He arrives at a conclusion through his experience (one that has been reached by all those who through the centuries have trusted God) in the form of a question: "Will not the God of all the earth do right?" (Genesis 18:25).

He was fully prepared to say without qualification that whatever happens on this earth, God will have done what is right and just. This fact is what every believer can fall back upon whenever faced with something they don't fully understand. This is the kind of faith that one possesses after years of experience, although probably not in the earliest years of faith's apprenticeship.

The Psalmist David was in no doubt that whatever happened in life (plenty of bad news came his way), God could be relied upon to be both righteous and loving in all that He does (Psalm 145:17).

The New Testament writers also shared this confidence in

the character of God. Jesus affirmed that God is kind to the ungrateful and the selfish (Luke 6:35) and that the rain was made to fall upon the just and the unjust (Matthew 5:43–45). The Apostle Paul asserted that God's kindness was meant to lead us to repentance (Romans 2:4).

With this conviction as our beginning assumption, we may now ask what happens to those who have never heard the name of Jesus. Whether or not we ever discover the perfect answer to this question, we may be at rest that God has always been, and always will be, both just and kind. God may be expected in every situation to do what is right and good. What prevents us from believing that the Creator of all that exists is far more just, far more merciful, and far more intelligent than we usually think?

There is no fairer or more just Being in all the universe than God, for righteousness and justice are the foundation of his throne (i.e., the basic pillars and principles of God's rule and reign [Psalm 89:14]). Moreover, in our sinfulness and distorted vision, we will never be in a position to judge the actions or decisions of our Creator.

There are still a few more hints in the New Testament we can factor in to our thinking. For example, in the third chapter of First Peter, there is a mysterious passage which forms the basis for the statement in the Apostles' Creed that, after his crucifixion and before his resurrection, Jesus descended into hell:

> He was put to death in the body but made alive by the Spirit, through whom also he went and preached to the spirits in prison who disobeyed long ago when God waited patiently in the days of Noah while the ark was being built.
>
> 1 Peter 3:18–20

No one really knows exactly what this passage means. In

every century since it was first penned, commentators have taken a stab at its interpretation. It triggers the imagination to ponder what Jesus was doing in the short period between his death and resurrection. One theory is that Jesus descended into hell to proclaim the knowledge of salvation to all who lived prior to his saving work. No other references suggest to us what occurred in these critical hours.

While we don't know exactly what occurred in those hours, we can understand that much was happening in all dimensions we are still unaware of. God was doing things behind the scenes completely unknown to us. However, the statement that Jesus went to preach to the spirits in prison before his resurrection does give us reason to think that the issue of fairness and justice to those who lived prior to Jesus was in God's mind before it was in ours. Our questions of right and wrong do not catch God off guard. The epitome of justice cannot be called into question by our mediocre and halfhearted standards of truth and righteousness. We may assume that if the matter of justice is to be raised at all, it does not originate with us.

Also, it makes sense to think that if Jesus did preach the Gospel of salvation to those who had no opportunity to hear it, there may be a great variety of other ways of declaring the Gospel to such people which God never needs to share with us. What we are told clearly is to do everything in our power to make the Gospel known to all those of our generation (Matthew 28:19–20). Only God can fill the role of God. We can't.

Ultimately, if Jesus is the only way to God, there will always be people in situations and in regions of the world we can't easily categorize. For all those dwelling on the earth for whom an answer is not immediately evident, we may fall back upon the ultimate wisdom and justice of God. Whatever else we may guess or think, we may say confidently about them,

"Last seen in the hands of God." We may go along fully with the trust of the patriarch Abraham, "Will not the God of all the earth do right?"

(3) Can't we measure religions by the good they produce?

Is a religion judged by its fruit? In a way, yes, and in another way, no. In the first place, we must ask what questions the religion hopes to answer. Most of the world's religions claim to answer the question, "What is the truth of my existence?" Whether we are talking about Hinduism, Islam, Buddhism, Judaism, or anything else on the spiritual scene, most (not all) are attempting to provide answers for issues such as why we exist, how we got here, what it all means, and where we are going. Some are merely trying to tell us what we should be doing along the way, even if they are not particularly bothered about our future existence. In any case, whatever questions they do consider, the answers are light years from being essentially the same.

The crucial question is: Does the particular religion give us a true account of our existence? Everything else is secondary. When we look at the practical good it does, it tells us something about its real worth. If you ask what faith has done the most good for the greatest number of people in history, the answer is the faith that is true.

If you believe that the greatest faith is the one that has done the most earthly good, then the path of investigation will lead to the same faith which ranks the issue of truth as primary. The person who seeks the true faith and the person who seeks the most helpful faith will cross paths in the end. That end is the truth and the kindness of Jesus Christ, the Son of God.

It is beyond dispute that the Gospel of Jesus has led to

the creation of more orphanages for the abandoned, more asylums for the destitute and disturbed, more hospitals for the sick, more feeding stations and rescue missions, more institutions of learning, more help for the poor or ravaged, more reform for prisons than any other faith, ever.

What the various religions of the world have learned in terms of helping people in practical ways has been taught to them largely by churches and missionaries. Wherever people have been left on the streets to starve and die, where the wounded have been untreated or children exposed to the elements to survive on their own, it can be safely said that there the Gospel of Jesus has not been allowed to take root.

To confirm these claims, there are two roads open: either read history or travel across the world. The facts are too numerous and too obvious to avoid. The record of Christianity's positive impact upon the physical, emotional, and spiritual needs of the world is so far beyond that of other religions that there's no comparison whatsoever. Where the Gospel of Jesus is planted, there the quality of life goes up, and where it's not permitted to thrive, or where it withers, the quality of life goes down.[1]

Finally, an interesting irony may be observed. Those religions which teach that salvation depends upon doing good works (this includes nearly all of them), don't really produce many. It's not where these religions thrive that you see the good fruit that you would expect. The greatest results of faith in terms of good fruit (meeting human need) are produced by those who do not depend upon them for salvation. Believers in Jesus are convinced that salvation is by grace and mercy alone, independent of any good works. It cannot in any way be achieved by doing good things. What good is done is not in the interests of earning salvation, but in grateful response to the salvation they have received as a gift from God.

(4) How can people who act so hypocritically be of the only true faith? Aren't all church people just hypocrites?

Hypocrisy is one of the most difficult things in life for us to accept. We have little tolerance for it and are quick to pronounce judgment, unless of course it is in reference to our own. In that case, we grant it wide latitude with plenty of elaborate excuses and denials. It is one moral flaw observed universally among the human family but discovered most often in our neighbor.

So the short answer to the question is yes. Every church person in every church is a hypocrite. Not a single one lives up to the claims or standards they profess. This is because every human being on earth is a hypocrite. Every man, woman, and child ever born has been the same in this one respect. Because we are all "fallen" creatures, we all suffer from the same malady. We make professions of all kinds, we claim to follow this standard or that, we try to live according to a pathway or commitment, but in the end we all fall short of even our most sincere intentions. We constantly overestimate what we are going to do or accomplish and how faithful we are going to be to our beliefs. This is just the nature of human life. Some people manage to do better or worse in this regard, but the same reality exists for all.

What makes faith in Jesus different here is that this is exactly what he expects of us. He does not expect or demand that we make ourselves better than we are or do better than we can before he accepts us. He states clearly in his teaching that if we try to live the life of faith on our own strength or by our own means, we are destined to fail miserably.

He taught that unless we dwell in his word and strength and draw from his power as the branch draws life from the vine, we will never produce one bit of fruit in life, at least the kind that he requires of us (John 15:1–5). We may manage to get rich, famous, or comfortable, but we will never become the kind of people he expects us to become.

To the pastor who hears the common complaint, "I couldn't possibly come to your church, or any church, because they're all so full of hypocrites," let me suggest this response:

> Hypocrites?! Is that your best shot? You don't know the half of it, my friend! If you have an hour or so, sit down and let me tell you about all the disordered personalities, misfits, malcontents, criminals, con artists, sociopaths, neurotics, psychotics, narcissists, kleptomaniacs, thieves, liars, swindlers, charlatans, predators, perverts, fugitives, rumor mongers, slanderers, clergy killers, bigots, racists, petty dictators, addicts, and a whole host of others in this human zoo we call the church – a cross section of broken humanity. Hypocrites? They're not our biggest problem!

Since the Gospel claims to be medicine for the sick, the church is where hypocrites can come and be forgiven and healed. They can gather together just as sick people come to the hospital and get well together. The more they worship together, pray together, study together, and love one another together, the more they will leave their illnesses behind and become less and less hypocritical. They do get better over time.

It must be remembered, too, that when the word "Christian" is used here, it does not refer mainly to a church person. It means someone who has come to a place of new birth, a transaction whereby Jesus Christ the Son has become the Lord and Master of all life. Churches are full of people who have never given themselves to Jesus in this respect and have no real knowledge of Father or Son. The church cannot be adequately judged purely by its official members, but by its Lord and his true followers.

Nevertheless, we have the right to expect more from Christ's true followers than from others. Jesus really does make a difference in our lives if we are truly dependent upon his merits and powers and not upon our own. If a person doesn't demonstrate in some way a quality of life which reflects his or her Lord, then something is broken that needs to get fixed.

(5) How could anyone's deep religious sincerity lead to judgment and hell?

In answering this question, the first thing to think about is whether on the human, earthly level – apart from any questions about heaven and hell – there is or has ever been a situation where absolute sincerity has led to death and destruction.

The answer isn't hard to find. What immediately comes to mind is the terrible period of world history when National Socialism threatened to take over all civilization. We are reminded of the days when thousands of unsuspecting Jews were taken out of the ghettos of Warsaw and shipped in cattle cars to the extermination camps. The Nazis persuaded the people to cooperate with their own demise by telling them that they were merely being moved to another location where there would be better conditions, or that they were being set free entirely. Many of the wealthier Jews actually bribed the guards for places on the trains hoping to get their families out first.

History tells the rest. As sincerely as they believed they were escaping to safety and survival, they ended up in an earthly hell. What they believed to be true was a lie, and what they firmly hoped for proved to be a fatal delusion.

We must ask ourselves this blunt question: Does what I

think or believe about something make any difference as to what is real or true? The answer must be an unqualified no. What is, is. We may wish things to be other than they are, but that wish doesn't have the slightest impact upon reality.

Our most firm and sincere belief in the nonexistence of hell will have no effect on whether or not it exists. Our happy confidence that all people everywhere will end up in a pleasant place after life is wholly irrelevant to the facts. The reality of hell comes to us on the authority of Jesus himself, so that if he really turns out to be the person he claimed to be, then the authority for the things he said follows logically. The true identity and status of Jesus and the certainty of hell are bound up together.

We have learned the lesson on many different levels and in many different generations that sincerity by itself means absolutely nothing. And if this lesson has been learned anywhere, it has been learned best in the study of the world's religions.

(6) If there really is a hell, what is it?

Most of our imagery of hell probably comes from medieval art and literature, but the New Testament itself doesn't give us a unified picture of it. We are never actually told exactly what hell is like. There is a variety of images used in Scripture to communicate that there is one and that it is to be avoided at all costs. The various mental images are used not so much to portray a literal picture of it, but more to convey a horror of it. A mixture of word-pictures such as fire, destruction, darkness, separation, emptiness, smoldering garbage dumps, and the like is utilized to create a revulsion to it, but the individual pictures can't put together a detailed visual description of it. Jesus said more about it than anyone else in the New Testament (e.g., Matthew 5:30; 13:40–43, 49–50; 18:7–9; Mark 9:42–48; Luke 13:22–30; John 3:16–21), but he never elaborated on the details. So we probably shouldn't say more about hell than Jesus did.

We are not encouraged by the New Testament to try to imagine exactly what it looks like, but we are vigorously exhorted to do everything and anything to keep from going there. This means to bow our knee in happy submission to the One who has done all that is required to secure our eternal rescue. People go there not because they failed to join a church or become a "good church person," but because they refused to have their sin problem dealt with. The seriousness of sin (our stubborn desire for independence from God and His will) should not be measured by our own cheerful evaluations of it but by its consequence, namely, eternal destruction.

The only way this problem can be treated is through the cleansing transformation of what Jesus calls rebirth. This is available for all who will accept it through what Jesus did on the cross. We cannot pay for it or earn it because it has already been paid for by Jesus himself.

People don't go to hell because they happened to be born in the wrong part of the world, but because they turn from the only light there is. It's the only place left to go for anyone who prefers darkness over light. What happens to those who resolutely refuse His presence? They are granted their desire and given His absence (or in the view of some theologians, His wrathful presence). Hell is the absence of all that is good. So it's not the case that God casts into hell people who want to be in His kingdom. On the contrary, there will be no one there who preferred the pleasure of His company.

Whatever hell is, it was never created out of God's good pleasure. It's the one place God has done everything possible to keep His people out of and has made every provision for them to avoid. Such is the meaning of Jesus' life, death, and resurrection. There is only one way for the sin problem to be dealt with and cured. There is only one way, one clear way, one absolutely indispensable way, for us to come home and be with our Creator forever.

(7) Why do we hear from so many church leaders today that Jesus is not the only way, but that he is the "best way" or the "only way for me"?

Prominent church leaders are finding that claiming Jesus to be the only way to God and salvation is just too unpopular. Some feel very uncomfortable making such an exclusive claim in our all-inclusive culture, and others simply don't believe it themselves.

Our seminaries are full of professors who don't believe that Jesus is the unique Son of God and are hostile to the idea that there could be just one way to God. Many of them seek to maintain their standing in the academic community in order to further their careers, and the fastest way to end an academic career is to state that Jesus is the incarnate Son of God who is the only Savior of the world. These professors then pass along their unbelief or skepticism to their students who imagine that this is what any truly up-to-date, thinking person should believe.

Denominational leaders are frequently those who have been promoted to high executive positions (within their respective denominations) just because they hold to a more universalistic view. Yet sitting in the pews of many congregations are those who hold to the biblical view and who, it is thought, need to be placated and patronized by the "enlightened" officials. Religious leaders will come out with statements such as, "He may be the only way for me/us, but we cannot say dogmatically that he must be the way for the

Hindu, the Buddhist, or the Muslim," or, "He is the very best way we know."

Those in the pew seem to believe these explanations more and more, but they make little sense and are far more difficult to defend than just saying outright, "Jesus is a fraud!" For reasons we've already discussed, the idea that every belief system is equal to every other, or that Jesus is relevant to some people but not to others, is the least intellectually respectable view available. It is the quintessential postmodern confession which attempts to hold mutually exclusive and contradictory views together without having to reconcile them with fact, logic, or reason. It's an abandonment of reason in favor of politics. To be sure, it's a great crowd-pleaser, but it doesn't survive rigorous cross-examination.

In recent days, a variation of this theme has been introduced by leading church officials and seminary professors who say, "Jesus is the only way to God alright, but he also saves by means of other religions. His work on the cross is so powerful and all-encompassing that it extends to those of other faiths whether followers of those religions are conscious of it or not."

This idea appears to be gaining in popularity in many traditional religious circles, even among conservative, evangelical believers. It has the advantage of retaining the biblical insistence that Jesus is the only road to salvation, but it appears to relieve the stress and strain of leaving out of the kingdom great numbers of the world's people. As such it's very attractive. To many who desire to be faithful to the historic Christian faith but who feel a natural compassion for all the peoples of the world, it appears on the surface to be the answer to our toughest questions about God. But is it?

There are at least two very big problems associated with this view:

(1) It's very hard to find any biblical evidence for it, and

(2) It results in removing the need for personal character transformation and eliminates the role played by ethics and morals in faith.

To begin with, if we regard the Scriptures as any authority on such matters, then we have to ask if there is anything in the Bible that suggests that Jesus saves through other faiths. There were at least as many different faiths in Jesus' day as in ours, so we have the right to ask that if such a belief were true, wouldn't it have been fairly obvious at least to some of those who wrote the New Testament?

But there doesn't appear to be a single hint of this in any one of the writings. We are told repeatedly that outside a saving relationship with Jesus Christ there is no salvation for any person. This was affirmed by the writers with reference to all the other religions present in the known world, including that faith in which Jesus himself was raised. Jesus instructed his disciples to go and make disciples of his in every village, city, and nation on earth. Why would he have given such a command if entirely unnecessary?

If his saving work could have been mysteriously implemented through the other religions of his day, then what would have been the point of any of his commands to go and declare his unique saving work to all the highly sincere believers of other faiths? Through his ongoing presence in the church, why would he have led his disciples into the teeth of every form of savagery and death as missionaries of this new faith?

Life outside direct and overt faith in Jesus is referred to in the New Testament not as a lesser form or level of light, but as "darkness" (John 3:19–20; 2 Corinthians 4:6; Ephesians 5:8). The language of light and darkness is also what is most frequently heard from those who come to Jesus from other faiths. We don't usually hear from such converts that they moved from one light to another light and finally to the greatest light, but rather that they came out of the darkness into the only light.

Secondly, the view abolishes the need for personal transformation as well as for ethical and moral action. In the New Testament it's very clear that the presence of Jesus among people is evidenced by definite personal spiritual growth and a resulting (and observable) new quality of life (Galatians 5:19–24; Ephesians 4:25–32). Jesus indicated that those whose lives were touched by him would be known to others by their fruit (Matthew 7:15–20; John 15:16). They would exhibit certain behavior and habits in line with his own and were commanded to love both neighbor and enemy in a radically new way (Matthew 5:44; 22:39). For him the quality of earthly ethical life mattered! All this was tied up with conscious obedience to his revealed will.

Jesus' disciples were to be like him in word and deed, but only to the extent that they were receiving from him the power to do so. Without him they could do nothing (John 15:5). Certain qualities of life were expected of all those in whom Christ's Spirit dwelt, and without this divine signature of new behavior they would never even see the kingdom of God (Galatians 5:21; Ephesians 5:5; Hebrews 12:14). Those in whom such things didn't exist were considered counterfeit believers who had no real connection with Jesus (Matthew 7:21–23; 25:31–46).

So when this new form of universalism is applied to the world of religion in general, it creates enormous problems with those religions which take no notice of sexual indulgence or abuse of women and children, which disregard justice and fairness, which foster hatred, violence, and indifference to the suffering of others, and the like.

If the theory were true that Jesus somehow extends his saving work into and through the religions of the world, then what would such a process of indirect salvation through Jesus look like? How would we describe this invasion of Jesus' saving power into the ideas and practices of other faiths? Surely we'd have to include all the religions, not just some, as we suggested previously. We can't choose just a handful of select or favorite faiths and declare them to be force fields of salvation while denying the same to others.

If so, we'd be faced once again with the same overwhelming intellectual, moral, and ethical dilemmas mapped out in an earlier chapter. In the end, it would mean that it really wouldn't matter in the slightest how we treated other people, what we did, or what we thought, so long as everything was done in the name of our religion. Jesus would manage to save us no matter what. We would even find ourselves affirming the salvation of those who openly repudiate Jesus and all that he stands for by doing everything in their power to block the open declaration of his name and to punish those who were attempting to do so.

Let's face up to the hard realities of where this view ultimately leads us. Do we really want Caligula, Hitler, Goebbels, Stalin, the Grand Inquisitor, or the endless list of religious terrorists and cruel tyrants to end up lavishly rewarded in Jesus' eternal paradise? Should they be there just because they were sincerely dedicated to their deeply held faiths and wholly given to the atrocities to which their beliefs led them?

Or, should we think that all the kind and nice people of every faith end up in God's presence no matter what they believe or do? But, as discussed elsewhere, this provides no real escape from our problems (see question 22).

In short, the difficulties mount up and become so great that innumerable subjective qualifications and exceptions need to be made in order to fit the facts into the theory. But by then there's very little left. Sure, the idea sounds good. It feels good to say it. It appears to ease the discomfort created by the unique claims of Jesus. Yet it leads us into total moral chaos. We are left only with a fuzzy "everythingism" with a shadowy and nondescript Jesus at the center.

(8) Why can't we all worship God in our own way?

We can and we do. This is already happening. We claim to worship God, the "gods," the "god within us," or some such thing in a variety of ways of our own making. The real questions are these: Is there a God out there who really exists, who really has a plan and purpose for us, and who wants us to worship Him in the way He requires? Has this God revealed Himself to us in any clear way, and does He declare that some things are acceptable to Him and some things are not?

Jesus' answers to these questions are that there are some facts we need to know about this God (his Father) and that we need to worship and serve Him in the way He has prescribed. According to Jesus, we cannot worship or serve Him properly by constructing our own homemade religions or attempting to please Him by doing the things He hates and refraining from doing the things He loves.

We cannot please and honor this God, for example, by taking showers in hot bull's blood, engaging in temple prostitution, ruthlessly murdering those who disagree with our theology, feeding rats while allowing children to starve, or a host of other forms of human behavior which God calls "evil" or an "abomination." Least of all can we please God by rejecting the one clear declaration of Himself through Jesus His Son and creating our own definition of Him.

According to Jesus, God hates all forms of idolatry and

wickedness, and by His holiness and purity He decrees that no one will ever see His kingdom without being qualified to do so. The only thing which qualifies us to enter is His sovereign decree from the foundation of the world. His plan is to bring us from whatever far country of self-reliance and self-worship we dwell in and usher us into His presence by invitation. We enter the divine palace through the single doorway of His will and are escorted in by the worthiness and merits of His only Son.

(9) Isn't the crucifixion of Jesus just another example of a bloodthirsty deity demanding human sacrifice?

There is a fairly popular argument among some skeptics which takes various forms, but may be stated briefly in the following way: If the New Testament claims that we are saved only by the "blood of Jesus," then how is this any different from all the other religions of the ancient world which describe a God with bloody hands? What kind of God would demand the cruel and bloody death of His only Son?

This is not such a bad question and occurs even to the devout believer in salvation through the death of Jesus. It's important to recognize, however, the sleight of hand that often occurs behind the question. The finger of accusation is actually pointing in the exact opposite direction of the guilty. It's a way of "framing" God for what properly lies at the door of sinful humanity.

The first question we should raise is this: To whom did the idea of murdering innocent people first occur? The answer is: To human beings. The first slayer in biblical history was Cain, son of Adam and Eve, who slew his brother out of jealousy and hatred (Genesis 4:2–12). Violently shedding the blood of the innocent was not and never will be God's idea.

The second question is much the same. Who was responsible for shedding the blood of the Old Testament prophets who came to speak to the people for God? The answer, too, is much the same as for the first question: The people to whom the prophets came.

The third question follows. Who is responsible for the crucifixion of Jesus Christ? Again, the answer is: Those to whom Jesus was sent. The explanation of the death of Jesus throughout the New Testament is that blind, sinful, and cruel people (both Jew and Gentile) crucified Jesus. They murdered him. In fact, some of them did so out of their own religious fervor and devotion. They were intensely sincere in their misguided spirituality, for they thought – they were in no doubt whatsoever – that they were doing the very work of God.

However, even though God allowed people to do what they wanted to do, and what their religious convictions (or lack of them) motivated them to do, nevertheless God wrote their evil behavior into His own script to cause the play to come out the way He determined it should, even before the foundation of the world. They were permitted to act out their malice in the form of killing the most innocent person ever to walk the earth, but God in His own sovereignty was free to exploit their sin for His own purposes.

God decreed that the merciless death of His Son would be the flash point of merciful salvation for lost and sinful human beings. He could have done anything He wanted to do because He was God, but He chose to exploit the murder of His Son, to make it the raw material by which He constructed the salvation of the race. It was a way of saying, "If you kill my Son, as you have my prophets, then I will make this, the lowest act of which you are capable, the very thing that saves you."

This result in the events of Jesus' life and death is a fulfillment of the Scriptural pattern recorded in Genesis pertaining to the life of Joseph: *What people intended for evil, God intended for good* (Genesis 50:20). This is the blueprint for how God had already chosen to deal with human evil even from the earliest days of human history.

What more eloquent statement could God have made regarding the utter hopelessness of self-salvation, and the nature of pure grace and mercy in the role of human deliverance and salvation? He chose to use not our piety and religious performance to save us, but our folly and sin. This completely disarms us in our attempts to achieve salvation by means of religious good works, for the best that our human intentions could accomplish was to kill the Son of God. God in His wisdom and mercy determined to turn the murder of His Son into the very act of forgiveness to all who would come in humility to Him and trust wholly and completely in the divine accomplishment of our eternal rescue.

Therefore, the death of Jesus was made the payment of sin for all to whom death was due. In this way, while the accusation was entirely true that Jesus' life was snatched from him (Acts 3:15), nevertheless it was equally true that Jesus gave his life willingly for us (Mark 10:45). The two realities intersect for the purpose of our salvation, while giving all the credit to God and none to us.

Back to our original question: Who, then, has been caught with bloody hands? Sinful human beings. Who is guilty of the death of Jesus? We are. Who is it who loves the shedding of innocent blood? It is we and we alone, the highly religious humanity that we are. The devout impetus to shed innocent blood in the name of this or that faith continues to this very day in the routine slaughter of Jesus' followers worldwide. There is more of it now than in the ancient world.

Such treatment of Christians continues to clarify how far wide of the mark human religious devotion can go. This ongoing attack upon his "body," the church, continues to remind us of the death of Jesus. It is the accomplishments of his death that still stand as the focal point of salvation for all who will come in simple, childlike humility to receive the divine mercy. Such a plan is referred to as "amazing grace."

(10) What does the Bible-believing Christian say about the Old Testament atrocities, the Crusades, the Inquisition, and such things?

Good question! And no doubt about it – the Bible, more particularly the Old Testament, is full of the most horrendous things in recorded religious history. For the most part, however, they are only reported rather than approved. The Bible is very candid about what it reports, even when the bad news refers to its heroes. All history – secular and religious – is full of acts of cruelty, barbarity, and stupidity. That's the way history really was. To report only roses and blue sky would make us very suspicious of the Bible's credibility.

On occasion, God Himself is described as commanding entire towns and villages to be completely destroyed along with every living thing. This is a difficulty not only for the skeptic, but for the most loyal Bible believer. We usually don't like to talk much about it.

How can we understand all this in a fair and honest way? One thing we can do is to put more facts on the table. First, it's clear that a flood of great, perhaps even worldwide, proportions was planned and carried out by the God of the Bible (Genesis 6:1–7:24). Every living creature perished, except for a small remnant of people and animals. Later on, somewhat the same thing happened on a smaller and more local scale under the leadership of the wandering Hebrews. They were ordered by God to wipe out whole towns.

We are horrified by reading some of these accounts. We like to think that religion brings only good, peaceful, and happy things to life. A violent God is almost instantly rejected by our generation – didn't He say in His Ten Commandments, "You shall not kill"? (What He actually said was that we should not commit murder.) We are highly offended by a God who brings His judgments to bear on human history. But let's face it, we're also highly offended by a God who does *not*. Don't we constantly hear how impossible it is to believe in a loving and just God who allows so much evil to continue in the world? Whether God judges or refrains from judging, we still like to beat Him with both ends of the same stick!

Once again, while not every question can receive an answer which perfectly satisfies everyone, some things can be clarified by filling in the blanks with more facts.

When it comes to some form of religious violence, the principal question to be addressed to any faith is: Does it have any intrinsic connection to the faith? Namely, does it proceed from the heart of it, and is it an essential part of its observance? Is worship and service expected to take place by means of it? Is it done in compliance with or defiance of the faith? The disturbing – even revolting – religious rites and rituals mentioned earlier in this book were part and parcel of those religions. They were expressions of obedience to those faiths.

Clearly, the heart of the Old Testament faith does not require violence to sustain it. It's not an ongoing commandment of God as an expression of true worship. It appears that God temporarily used Israel as an instrument of His judgment upon the wickedness of towns and nations to provide a place for His people to settle and thrive. Without removing the offending people, there would have been no opportunity for the Hebrews to obey God's command to become a blessing and source of reliable information about God to all mankind.

The radical evil and aggression of the surrounding peoples prevented the Hebrews from even beginning to fulfill their divine commission.

What is surprising is that on some occasions when we would expect entire groups to be ruthlessly eliminated, they are spared and even blessed. One notable example is when an invading army, intent on committing great atrocities on God's people, surrounds the city where the prophet Elisha is staying. Instead of being destroyed, however, they are treated by God's prophet to a great feast, then sent away happy and well fed (2 Kings 6:8–23).

The policy of total destruction of some groups was apparently selective, temporary, and local. The goal was to clear away the land in preparation for the people of Israel to inherit what God had promised to his servant Abraham (Genesis 12:1–3). They were permitted – even ordered – to continue fighting against the wicked nations long enough to complete the task.

God is clearly portrayed as taking no pleasure in the death of the wicked (Ezekiel 33:11). Rather, He was refusing to tolerate forever their chronic violations of His basic laws of justice and order. The warlike and violence-loving nations, each with long histories of unbelievable brutality, received in turn the just reward for their own choices. To take no action against them would have allowed chaos and disorder to spread into ever-widening circles and, ultimately, to reign over the earth once again. Also, it must be remembered that just as God used His people to bring judgment upon the sins of the surrounding nations, so He used those nations as instruments of His judgment upon the Hebrews when they violated His law.

The Old Testament understanding of divine judgment was primarily the separation of chaos from order for the purpose of putting right-side up an upside-down world. It was carried out to maintain the goodness of God's original creation. His judgments were for the welfare of His creatures. God's superintendence over history in this way could be seen in much the same light as a referee's overseeing the progress of a sports event. Who among us would want to participate in a football game without an official on the field?

None of the violence toward humans in the Old Testament had any necessary connection to the ongoing worship of God. God didn't require the death of all those who preferred to avoid His presence and rule. He permitted nations to dwell for long periods of time in willful ignorance of, even open contempt for, His will and purposes for centuries thereafter and up to the present day.

As for the New Testament and the teaching of Jesus (the foundation of the Christian faith), we cannot find a single hint of instruction on the part of Jesus that violence and death are part of his continuing will for the church, or are in any way intrinsic to the worship of God. What things people have chosen to do in the name of Jesus Christ, whether foolish Crusades to acquire land or cruel Inquisitions to enforce institutional dogmas, have been entirely the dark decisions of those who apparently hadn't the slightest idea what Jesus actually taught.

Jesus spoke openly of those who would call him "Lord," but who refused to do or be what he really wanted and taught (Luke 7:21, 23). He said that the wheat and the weeds, the sheep and the goats, would dwell intermixed until he himself would come in the Final Judgment and separate them forever.

To summarize, the debauchery in the name of religion mentioned in an earlier section was regarded in each case as a form of obedience to the particular faith being described. Abhorrent acts were prescribed acts of worship. However, what is *prescribed* by the world's religions is *proscribed* by the teaching of Jesus. Any and all forms of depravity, violence, self-exaltation, and self-serving manipulation of others done in the name of Jesus are always in defiance of his revealed will.

(11) How can we be critical of people's deeply held religious beliefs?

Have you ever noticed that when the subject of religion comes up in public discussions, everything seems to change? A strange silence occurs. Normal conversation comes to a grinding halt. Seemingly by mutual agreement, all rules are suddenly suspended and what goes for every other question or issue is summarily tossed out the window. Eyes glaze over and absolute subjectivism takes control.

Whether it's a television interview or newspaper article, people's personalities are instantly transformed into something different. The fiercest film critic, the most dogmatic politician or passionate activist, the most brutal interviewer or hardened city newspaper editor suddenly becomes a toothless puppy! All critical objectivity is dropped, and an air of feigned reverence is adopted. They become opinionless. We begin to hear things like this:

- "We can't talk about religion the way we talk about other things."
- "I can't make judgments about people's most deeply held beliefs."
- "You don't have the right to evaluate someone's religion."

We hear these comments so often they seem to make sense to us.

The only exception to this is the way in which conservative, historic Christian faith is treated. It remains the only belief system that can be openly criticized or vilified without social penalty. When it comes to this system of "deeply held beliefs," all rules of civility and courtesy disappear. Toward the world's principal religions, people become painstakingly uncritical. However, when it comes to Christian faith, they become so hypercritical that they use standards they wouldn't anywhere else. But all this is to be welcomed. This faith is solid enough to survive the hammering.

Any faith (Christian or otherwise) is simply a claim to truth and is as much a declaration of truth as any political or philosophical school of thought. It *should* be open to critique. We never hear from a newspaper editor, "We can't criticize the ideas of the Democrats/Republicans because these are people's deeply held beliefs!" How often does a professor of political philosophy say to his students, "We make it a practice never to criticize Marxism or Capitalism because these are the cherished beliefs of many sincere people." We feel free to examine vigorously or even rip into the deeply held and cherished beliefs of others when it comes to every other department of life. But the word "religion" brings all critical analysis to a halt.

Since when do "deeply held beliefs" or "sincere ideas of truth" make any difference at all? Why should this give religion (any religion) a free pass? Any claim to truth should be subjected to the same criteria, analytical thought, and cross-examination as every other idea or claim. No other field of thought demands more of our critical thinking and highest level of reason.

As soon as we begin to apply our best deductive reasoning, logic, and rational standards to the study of the world's religions, we quickly recognize something interesting: People often come to their most deeply held beliefs on the flimsiest evidence and weakest standards of truth. Seasoned scientists who demand hard fact during their work day come to accept or reject ultimate issues of life, death, and eternity based on the most feeble claims.

History tells us that those who have had the courage to apply what they have learned about analysis and critical thinking to religious belief are often led by this very avenue to worship and serve Jesus Christ, the Son of God.

(12) Isn't it anti-Semitic to claim that Jesus is the only way?

This is the only question of the lot that really doesn't belong here, but it is included because it is so often encountered. The criticism would be regarded as unimportant if it weren't taken with such absolute seriousness by those who make it.

How could the claim about Jesus be anti-Semitic? Jesus was a Jew from Jewish parents, raised in Judaism, taught by Jewish standards, living out his life as a Jew and disputing with other Jews about Jewish teaching. Many Jews, including leading Jewish authorities, came to believe that he was the promised Messiah of the Old Testament. The very first followers of Jesus were Jewish, and the first churches were made up almost exclusively of Jews. The twenty-seven documents that preserved the teaching of Jesus were written by Jews, with only one possible exception. These followers died as Jews believing in Jesus as the incarnate Son of God.

They remained devout monotheists their entire lives and were absolutely committed to the Old Testament and the Ten Commandments. The Apostle Paul (Saul of Tarsus) was one of the best-educated Jewish thinkers of his time and wrote letters arguing that Jesus was the promised Messiah of God. This claim had only two logical possibilities:

(a) He was the Messiah

(b) He was not the Messiah.

These are exactly the lines along which the official Jewish response developed. Some said that Jesus was the Messiah, and some said that he was not. How can anyone squeeze anti-Semitism out of all this?

If Jesus was seen as a scandal by other Jewish leaders, this would have to be viewed as a theological squabble within Judaism, not as an attack upon it from without. No weaker claim could ever be made than that Jesus' teaching was and is anti-Semitic. How can a devout Jew be anti-Semitic? The complaint is in every respect an offense to reason and common sense.

No doubt the New Testament has been used in history to generate anti-Semitism by those who chose to hate the Jewish people, but so have various schools of philosophy, including Darwinism. If someone wants to be anti-Semitic, any idea will do. Anti-Semitism arises from within the heart of wicked people who will exploit any means necessary to justify their hatred and malice.

(13) Why can't all religions be viewed as just various solutions to the problem?

The reason why all religions can't be seen as multifaceted solutions to the basic problem of human existence and destiny is that, from the point of view of the Bible, religion *is* the problem. The very fact that human beings have sought out more and more religions to fill the vacuum of God's absence is the symptom of the problem to which Jesus Christ is the solution. Religion is the very thing God doesn't want! It's a symptom of the disease. We were created by God to be in a relationship with Him by means of His grace and mercy alone, not by means of religious observances or rule keeping. The introduction of religion into the life of human beings is the sign that from the start things had gone very wrong.

Jesus is the solution to the problem of sin. It is sinful rebellion and self-will which compels us to create religions of our own preferences to take the place of God. The fact that there is a variety of religions to choose from in the world is the most direct evidence that the problem is not fixed, but rather exacerbated.

In the same way that fellowship with God the Creator was offered and rejected in favor of "religion" by the descendants of Abraham, so the church of Jesus Christ throughout its history in large measure has been a reenactment of this. Any time God offers us a relationship, we respond by saying, "Thanks, we'll take a religion." It's just much easier and far more convenient that way. As long as we have a religion, we imagine we can remain in control of things. When we have a relationship, we admit God is in control.

Inevitably, the living faith of ancient Israel, based wholly upon the grace and free mercy of God as well as the living faith of the early church which emerged from it, gave way to the calcifying process of becoming a religion – an organization, an outward form without vitality and power. Even though Christian thinkers have tended to point the finger of accusation at Judaism for its development, nevertheless exactly the same thing has happened within Christianity. What started out as a living relationship of grace has in many places and in many ways hardened into just another religion. Such is the ever-present tendency of the rebellious human heart.

Thus, the problem: "sin." By definition it is the desire – the overpowering obsession – to remain in control of our own lives and destinies. It is the will to define for ourselves what is good and evil, true and false, right and wrong. It stubbornly resists the rule and reign of God over us at all points and is so powerful in its effects that it cannot be broken by sheer human willpower. It seeks to focus upon the trivial and the external while wholly avoiding the internal corruptions of the will and heart. It is a tyranny that no religious observance or following of rules can break. It is something which imprisons us and from which we must be delivered from the outside.

This deliverance is what has been claimed in Jesus, the strong Son of God. He comes to our prison, breaks through the gates and bars of all our religions, and leads us out. He brings us back home by virtue of his own merits and power.

(14) Which is it: faith in Jesus, or faith in God the Creator? How can we have it both ways?

When the New Testament speaks of faith, it usually refers to faith in Jesus Christ rather than in God the Father. In the overwhelming number of cases, Jesus Christ the Son is the object of the believer's faith. Why is this so? Clearly, it's not that the Son is considered more important than the Father or that the Father has been displaced by Jesus the Son. Nor can it be said that we are to worship two gods. On the contrary, the Apostle Paul tells us that at the end of time, when the work of Jesus the Son is forever completed, he will hand over the entire kingdom to the Father (1 Corinthians 15:24).

The answer lies in the fact that no one can claim to have faith in the one true God without first going through the Son. One can't go around Jesus the Son and still hope to arrive at God the Father, the Creator of all things. Therefore, to have faith in the Son is at the same time to have faith in the Father, and to have faith in the Father is to recognize His Son. This is the intended order of things (1 John 2:23–24; 5:1).

It's not possible, then, to claim an interest in, love for, or trust in God, while at the same time ignoring or bypassing the Son. We just can't have God the Creator while avoiding or evading His beloved Son. Jesus Christ is always the single entryway into the presence of the Father.

(15) Why do Christians hate people of other religions?

It's remarkable that there are many people who think that Christians hate people who believe differently from them. I'm sure it's true that there are those who really do hate and fear people of other religions, but it's not true that they are Christians.

By definition, those who hate others can't be considered Christians at all, for love of God and hatred of one's neighbors are not able to dwell in the same heart. We are told that sweet and bitter water can't flow from the same well (James 3:11). The New Testament makes this very clear. Whatever we imagine ourselves to be, we cannot be genuine followers of Jesus while at the same time hating our enemy (Matthew 5:43–44; Luke 6:27; 1 John 2:9). We would be wholly deluded.

The Christian attitude toward people of other religions is absolute, unqualified acceptance, love, and respect for the person, but at the same time a firm rejection of all ideas which place Jesus Christ on any level other than that of eternal Son of God and the sole means of salvation for all mankind. Hostility, cruelty, hatred, even dislike or arrogance toward others because they believe differently is entirely out of place in the life of the Christian. It is itself a clear index of how far away from God we really are.

The true believer in Jesus is by nature a friend of the unbeliever. In the early days of the Christian faith, believers were known for the ease and quickness with which they would sacrifice their very lives and fortunes for the sake of those outside the faith. The church was known as the only society which existed largely for those who were not members of it. It was primarily the death of the early martyrs, particularly the way they died, in love and forgiveness toward their persecutors and executioners, that put an end to many of the strange accusations hurled at the Christians.

Believers within the Roman Empire were accused of hating the human race, loving to start fires, even engaging in cannibalism and all kinds of wild orgies. It was the existence of such reckless and irresponsible rumors which compelled Emperor Trajan to employ his investigative reporter to find out the truth of these matters. When the rumors were carefully scrutinized, the result proved to be for the benefit of the Christians. As it turned out, what hatred did exist was directed toward them.

People today who truly hate others for any reason and still wish to be regarded as Christians are those the early church would regard as false disciples. They are counterfeit Christians, irrespective of whatever else they believe or confess, or however pious they may appear. As any pastor knows, the Christian church in much of the world is filled with people who wish to be numbered among the lot of believers in Jesus, but who have never had a real encounter with the Lord of lords and King of kings. They have never had a rebirth experience of the kind mentioned in the New Testament (John 3:3–7) or gone through a transformation of the mind (Romans 12:2).

Jesus spoke of his church as the place where the wheat and the tares (weeds) will grow together side by side until the last day when the true and the false shall be separated forever (Matthew 13:24–29). In the meantime, it is God's kindness and patience, even toward the sinful within the church, that is meant ultimately to lead them to repentance and change (Romans 2:4).

(16) Why can't we see Jesus as just a great moral example to follow?

This is no doubt the exit route most people take when it comes to Jesus. We find it much more comfortable and manageable to view Jesus as a great moral teacher and fine example to follow in life (someone like Gandhi, Mother Theresa, or St. Francis) than as the incarnate God and Ruler of history. Yet this is not the product being advertised. Even though we're clearly told in the New Testament that we are to live life in imitation of Christ (Philippians 2:5; 1 Peter 2:21), it's also clear that this is regarded as humanly impossible.

The believer is taught to follow in the footsteps of Jesus and can accomplish this only with his help. This is possible only to those who live in a close relationship with Jesus and the Father. To those who have only a passing interest in Jesus, it is viewed as entirely beyond their reach (John 15:1–7).

Test this for yourself. For example, do you in your own strength bless those who hate you, or return good for evil to some enemy of yours? Do you give even more to those who steal from you or willingly turn the other cheek to someone who strikes you? Do you forgive those who persecute you, and would you, with your last breath, ask God not to hold your killers to account? Are you able to manipulate molecules so you can turn water into wine and multiply a few pieces of bread and fish into a lavish feast for thousands? If you're like the rest of us, such behavior is not something we can pull off on our own steam. If Jesus is only an "example" of what we are expected to emulate, then we are all in deep trouble.

Jesus is considered not merely the moral and ethical example to follow, but the prototype describing our destiny – the model of humanity which lies at the end of our journey of faith. He's the heavenly human, the "Second Adam" (1 Corinthians 15:45–49), who achieves what the first earthly

Adam failed to do. He lived the life not of the superhuman, but of the human. His astonishing moral and spiritual power, even his ability to perform miracles, was the result of his daily dependence upon the power of the Creator, his Father (John 5:16–21). In this way, he acted out human life as intended all along by the Creator.

The fact that we are infinitely far from living this kind of life is the greatest illustration that we are currently living not a human life, but a subhuman life. At present, we are broken and incomplete people. Haven't you ever wondered why those around you (or you yourself) were living so far below humanity's apparent potential, and behaving in a way so beneath how we should or could? The answer is that even though we are living this low-altitude life now, nevertheless as we are drawn ever closer into the life of Christ, we will become progressively more human. One day, at the end of our earthly road, we'll finally reach our destiny, not to become God or gods, but to become fully human. Jesus gives us a preview of what that human life will be like.

So it seems that the claims of Jesus are even more than we thought. He comes to us not only to reveal what God is like, but what all of us who follow him into the eternal kingdom of the Father will be like.

(17) Why don't the majority of professors, scholars, and intellectuals accept the exclusive claims of Jesus?

Firstly, we don't really know if this is true or not. It is difficult to get at the real figures since many top thinkers in each field are reticent to say what they personally believe about Jesus. Rarely an advantage in the academic world to confess faith in Jesus Christ, it's more often the professional kiss of death to do so. More than one career has been either cut short or severely limited by this open admission.

Secondly, as the case may be, suppose for the moment it's true that the majority do not accept Jesus' claims. That being so, we may also assume on similar grounds that the majority of plumbers, taxi drivers, repairmen, clerks, and waiters do not accept them either, at least not on any level of personal commitment. It really doesn't matter what one does for a living. It's truer to say that the majority of people in general opt out of Jesus' mastery over life simply because they don't want it – it doesn't fit their lifestyle or it gets in the way.

In talking with people about Jesus over the last 40 years, I've observed that whatever a person does for a living, be they a scholar or manual laborer, the likelihood of their ever considering Jesus' claims in a thoroughgoing, thoughtful manner is very low. Ignorance of the facts is high on the list of reasons why people don't accept the New Testament declaration of Jesus' identity.

If the theory behind the question is that there's a direct connection between intelligence or education and faith, then we can successfully debunk it. A quick search through all the available information reveals that some of the most brilliant and highly educated people in history have accepted the claims about Jesus. Many have come to faith just by investigating the abundant evidence available. Moreover, in the U.S. today, recent studies show that regular church attendance is just as likely in the higher educated circles as in the lower.[2]

One of America's most highly respected physicists (who understandably wants to remain anonymous) said that in his view nearly one half of all physicists in America he has come across in his travels are believers in Jesus, but are very low-key about it. However, the higher you climb the staircase of scientific power – namely, the positions of national influence and educational policy making – the more dramatically the percentage of believers plunges.

You are more or less expected to confess faith in evolution and the chance origins of the universe to be fully accepted in the halls of scientific political power. In other words, in the realm of physics, as in other scientific fields (particularly biology), there seems to be an unwritten rule regarding the "survival of the most Darwinian."

(18) How can Jesus be both human and divine? The church's doctrine of the Trinity is just too hard to swallow.

If you find the church's doctrine of the Trinity too hard to swallow, then don't swallow it. Rather, as you move carefully through the biblical evidence, let it emerge naturally and gradually as it did to Christianity's earliest thinkers. It was formulated by intelligent people of various times and places seeking to arrive at some coherent summary of the raw biblical data. It seemed to its formulators inescapable to say that God must be in three separate persons while existing as one substance. There are not three Gods, but one God, a three-in-one unity: God the Father, God the Son, and God the Holy Spirit. Many have tried to do a better job of putting the evidence together. Thus far no one has been successful.

If we try to explain it on our own, we must make sure the definition does full justice to the facts as presented in the texts about Jesus and his relationship to the Creator – including all the affirmations and claims about him found in chapter two. What we must avoid at all costs is saying things like, "God couldn't, wouldn't, or shouldn't be or do that!" If God exists at all, we may assume that He is what He is and may disclose Himself however He pleases. Who are we to say what God must or must not be like?!

God's intent in the coming of His Son in the form of flesh

and blood was to allow us to put a face to Him. Haven't you ever said, "I know the name, but I can't place him"? We can know God's name, understand the meaning of the affirmations about His being all-powerful, everywhere present, always existing with no beginning or end, and all the rest. But all this is just too enormous for our minds to take in. If the universe as we know it is too gigantic even to imagine, then how far greater is the God who made it. This vastness makes God too abstract, too impersonal, and too distant. Now, not only do we know His Name, but in the God-man, Jesus of Nazareth, we can put a face to God. It was one of God's greatest ideas!

How can Jesus be both human and divine? None of us knows exactly how. There's no one else around to compare with.

(19) How can we take the Bible literally in this day and age?

The real problem with this question is that it's not always easy to figure out what it means. What specifically is intended by it? For example, a church member told his pastor, "I don't take the Bible literally, but I do take it seriously." But what does it mean to take something literally? We see the problems using such language creates when we ask the same question of other writings. Should we take Shakespeare literally? Should we take the works of Roman historians Suetonius or Pliny literally?

The same fuzzy thinking carries over to the typical college or university course, "The Bible as Literature." Have we ever seen a course listed as "Shakespeare as Literature"? What else could it be but literature?!

The fact is that the Bible is literature and nothing but literature in its many forms: history, poetry, letters, gospels, parables, apocalyptic (Revelation, for example), and so forth. Much of it is metaphorical or symbolic in nature, and much is historical or poetical in nature. Some biblical language is meant to evoke a response, some meant to report history, some to describe, some to spark the imagination, and some to inspire. Each must be interpreted according to the kind of literature being read at any given time. We interpret poetry in one way, apocalyptic or prose in another, and history in still another.

If something is intended metaphorically, it ought to be understood metaphorically. If something is intended historically, it should be understood as such. We would be foolish to take a statement in some symbolic way if it was intended by the writer to be a literal statement, just as it would be ridiculous to interpret literally what was intended poetically.

Very simply put, we take metaphors as metaphors, symbols as symbols, euphemisms as euphemisms, and literal statements as literal statements. This is something we do every day without even noticing it. To do anything else would mean confusion at best and total disaster at worst. If the highway sign ahead reads "Bridge Washed Out," then we need to apply our best reasoning and conclude that we should interpret this exactly as intended.

When it comes to the Bible, we should either take it the way it was intended by the original writers (as far as it can be determined), or not take it at all. If Luke tells us that Jesus and the disciples entered the city of Jericho, then we should understand that they entered the city of Jericho. If we just can't accept that Jesus transformed water into wine at the wedding party, or on Easter morning Jesus rose bodily from the dead, then we are bound by honesty and intelligence to toss the claims out altogether. We have no obligation (or right) to understand them in some metaphorical way. They either happened that way or they didn't. Historical statements are true or false. There is no in-between.

Of course, in some instances in both the Old and New Testaments, the author's original intent is not absolutely clear to us today. However, in such cases, no key or essential tenet of faith hangs in the balance.

Outright rejection of the Bible's authority is far superior to qualified acceptance of it based upon the assumption that we can interpret it any way we please. If we tried to drag the tired old horse of personal subjectivism into our course on Shakespeare or Roman History 101, we would undoubtedly leave with an "F" on our transcript. The academic dean would expect us to interpret that grade as literally as possible!

(20) Isn't this story about Jesus a bit too simple?

The story about Jesus and salvation through him alone is indeed simple. In fact, it's the most straightforward, uncomplicated story ever told about human life and destiny. No simpler explanation of where we came from, what human life on earth means, and where we are going after death can be found anywhere.

But how else would we have it? Do we really want the highly complex and suspect explanations of life and death which many of the religions of the world offer us? Do we actually prefer the elaborate systems of belief given to us by, let's say, ancient Gnosticism, one of the hottest competitors of the Christian faith in the early centuries of its existence? This religious system was so difficult to understand that only a select few of the elite were ever capable of grasping it or qualifying for its supposed benefits.

Going back to our earlier discussion on the bewildering smorgasbord of religious options on the market, so radically different one from the other, doesn't it make perfect sense to suppose that the answer would be a simple one? Don't we hear ourselves complaining, "Why doesn't God just spell it all out for us and make Himself perfectly plain?" If there really were a God who cared at all for His creatures, wouldn't He go out of His way to make the most important questions in life clear and easy for all to grasp? Why would this God make things so difficult to access that only a few could ever reach it?

The only message that could be received by the billions of diverse people on the planet by its nature would have to be a simple one. The university professor of philosophy, the auto mechanic, the waiter, the street sweeper, the mentally retarded, the little child, and everyone in between are offered a message from the Creator which cuts across all boundaries of intellect, race, age, culture, and mental capacity.

The only prerequisite to taking the decisive step from death to life and from darkness to light is the desire to be forgiven and welcomed home by our Creator. Everything needed to secure our eternal salvation has been accomplished by Jesus, the only Son of God. That's how simple it is.

(21) Isn't it trying to play the role of God to say that Jesus is the only way?

Agreed! It would be trying to play the role of God if believers in Jesus were the ones who cooked up the idea in the first place. But what if the claims of Jesus were true, and it really was God's idea, not theirs? Surely, no one can presume to play the role of God, but can't God choose to play the role of God? This is exactly what the Gospel of Jesus declares: God took the initiative to reveal Himself in the clearest possible way in His Son, Jesus.

What followers of Jesus are saying is that they unequivocally believe the declaration of Jesus. They argue that all the
available evidence indicates it is true and we are in great peril
in willfully disregarding it. In the act of proclaiming it to
others, they are simply obeying the command of their Lord
to do so.

(22) Why don't all good people go to heaven?

This, probably the most common question asked by
inquirers, has been reserved for last. It seems to make so
much sense. Why would any person of whatever land and of
whatever creed be ultimately excluded from the presence of
God when, for all practical purposes, they lived a perfectly
good and upright life? Why would a good God reject the
obviously good person?

Why indeed?! The answer isn't far away. The natural
follow-up question is simply this: Who is truly good, and who
is the definer of that good? It depends upon whom you ask,
doesn't it? For some, the good person is the "nice person,"
the one who is friendly, helpful, loving, kind, and gentle. To
another, the good person is the one who is the most dedicated
to their religion and its requirements. For many religions of
the world, both ancient and modern, this would indicate the
person who most consistently, thoroughly, and devotedly
carried out the goals of their faith. These could easily include
the brutal murder of those who disagreed with their creed,
the enslavement of other races and tribes, human sacrifice,
child molestation, cruel torture of perceived enemies, world
domination, and on and on. See the problem?

Good compared to what? That's the question. "Well," you
might answer, "I mean the person who has never engaged in
the bad things mentioned above – who is always nice and

kind to everyone and hurts no one." But, it may be asked, who are you to say what is good and what is not? Your definition is just as exclusive as that of any other faith. Those who have another standard of good and try their best to live up to it with all sincerity are excluded from your paradise. Without some absolute standard by which to measure, how can you offer this restriction upon others who are just as sincere in their beliefs as you are?

Also, how do we really know how good someone else is, regardless of what they appear to be? Haven't you ever been fooled by people who seemed very good on the outside, but turned out in the end to be envious, proud, greedy, arrogant, cruel, elitist, racist, and all the rest? What about salespersons, politicians, ministers, and friends you thought were good and trustworthy and, in actual fact, were anything but.

The New Testament teaches that a relative goodness from one person to another is possible (which God recognizes), but we all, without exception, have a "sin nature." It has been there from the beginning of time – from the beginning of life itself – dwelling within each of us, whether we are (or appear to be) better or worse than our neighbor. Ultimately, we are to be compared not to one another, but to the absolute standard of God's purity and holiness. In comparison to this standard, we all fall tragically and profoundly short. We come nowhere near the passing grade of God's perfection because it's just not in us.

I know "good people" and "bad people," and so do you. There's a great variety of human beings in this world, and we can be as radically different from one another as humanly conceivable. When we get to know each other individually, we always see a side of our character which eventually is revealed in one circumstance or another. I observe your dark side, and you observe mine – normally, we are street smart enough not to be surprised by this. We remain friends (hopefully) because we don't expect total perfection in each other.

The New Testament says that without holiness we will not see the Lord (Hebrews 12:14). But we've just learned that we're not holy and can't be on our own. The good news is that God knows this perfectly well and doesn't expect us to achieve holiness by our own efforts. He knows that our best attempts to "become good" end either in discouragement and failure or (for some who are convinced that they've succeeded) insufferable pride. This was one of the primary lessons learned by the monks during the monastic movement of the early centuries of the church. These most honest souls who actually tried to achieve holiness and moral purity found that, when they really took a long look inside themselves, they were more or less just the same old moral weaklings they were when they started out.

What's the answer? It may be captured in the famous prayer of Saint Augustine, who really attempted to fulfill the moral law of God and found himself wanting. He realized that all the great commands of God were impossible to fulfill in any literal way. In his despair, he cried out the prayer of every human being who has ever tried to be good and failed: "Lord, give what you command." In other words, "Lord, I can't achieve your requirements for goodness, but you can do it for me and in me. Please grant me the power to do and be what you require."

God's answer to this kind of prayer is, "I thought you'd never ask!" God has already made provision for this in Jesus Christ, His Son. His sinless and perfect Son has done for us what we could not do for ourselves. He paid the price for our failures and sins. He absorbed into himself the penalty for our transgressions and offers us the free gift of salvation through him alone. All that was needed was done for us. What is expected of us is the humility to receive the gift and bow our knee in happy submission to the Lord of lords and

King of kings.

To turn down this offer in place of some paltry and pathetic attempt to become "good," to be acceptable in our own eyes and in the eyes of others, is judged by God as the height of folly and foolishness. It is the opposite of goodness; it is, in fact, the pinnacle of pride and defiance. Deliberately snubbing the Son of God in favor of our own self-righteousness or homemade "goodness" is the most vain and dark act we could ever be capable of, compared to which the violence and cruelty of misguided religious devotion is a virtue. The latter is forgivable. The former is not.

summary and conclusion

Let's summarize where we've been and what it all means. We began with the startling claim that Jesus Christ is the only way to God and salvation. Apart from him there is no way whatsoever. Most people today see it as the most preposterous claim anyone could ever make, saying, "It's just too narrow and bigoted for us to accept."

We reminded ourselves to be somewhat suspicious of our own ability to reason things out when our knowledge of the facts is very limited. If life teaches us anything, it is that we are prone to self-delusion of all kinds. What appears to be true or real very often proves, in the end, to be merely an illusion. Life presents us a series of mirages, and only time, more facts, and further experience can reveal to us the full scope of our predicament.

These illusions are reinforced by "postmodern thought" – imagined to be an advance in thinking, but which, in reality, is only a return to the primal sin of the first human beings. This thinking supposes that we can find refuge from our Creator. Yet we find that wherever we attempt to flee from the Lord of the manor, we are still on His land.

With these cautions in place about the way we think, we

asked a few basic questions about the claims of Jesus: Are they inherently unlikely? Or are we just thoroughly soaked in the current intellectual environment and unable to think for ourselves about them? We discovered that if we were to ask the question as we would any question about scientific fact, it wouldn't seem preposterous at all. The idea that there is one way and only one way to an end is perfectly in order when considering almost any other field of knowledge. There is no compelling reason why this should not apply in the realm of ultimate truth about God.

Next, we asked the question about the claims themselves: What exactly has been claimed about Jesus? We saw that they are far higher than usually even advertised. From the point of view of the New Testament, Jesus isn't just another prophet or religious leader on the scene, but the eternal co-Creator of the universe, who came in flesh to reveal who God the Father is and what a real human being is like. He lived a real human life, died a real death on a Roman cross, was buried and then raised to life in a transformed physical body, never to die again. He ascended to God the Father where he reigns over time and history, and from where he will return to judge humanity. Ultimately, he will pronounce an end to all evil and chaos, and create a new heaven and a new earth where righteousness and justice alone dwell.

No other human being in history ever made claims coming anywhere close to those of Jesus. If even 10 percent of his claims were regarded as authentic, they would still far transcend those of any other person in history.

There is every reason to believe that the astonishing claims about Jesus' identity and mission came from Jesus himself. No defensible argument exists to persuade us that they came from the naiveté of the disciples, or from the later church, who managed to lose touch with the original teaching of Jesus.

Moreover, we saw that the original writing of the primary documents of the faith are dated well within the lifetime of the earliest witnesses, thus protecting the documents from the accusation that bold fabrications, myths, and legends had been introduced into the texts when there was no one around to challenge or correct them.

We looked at the documents in which these claims have been preserved. We found that whatever historical questions we can direct toward them reveal that they can stand up under fire better than any other documents that have come down to us from the ancient world. The manuscripts are more in number, better attested, and closer to the events they claim to report than those which exist for the Greek or Latin classics we routinely accept.

We saw that the early Church Fathers made such extensive use of the Scriptures through quotes and allusions that virtually the entire New Testament could be reproduced even if not a single Greek manuscript had survived. This corroborative evidence has no real parallel with any other ancient literature.

We discovered that the historical information within the New Testament – the framework within which the Gospel is set – is demonstrably reliable and trustworthy. We know this through archeology and the historical sciences which should be regarded as friends, not enemies, of the Bible.

We considered the question whether the claims attributed to Jesus were merely legends and found that the evidence points in the exact opposite direction of what we commonly know about legends. Some of the highest statements about Jesus are also the earliest.

We looked at the resurrection of Jesus as the vindication of his claims and suggested further resources to support the view that the resurrection of Jesus is among the most well-documented events of the ancient world.

We considered the usual objections to these claims. The protest that matters pertaining to Jesus and eternal salvation are too important to be based merely upon historical evidence was seen to be unfair and arbitrary. Nevertheless, it was shown that the evidence for and proofs of Jesus' claims have a wider base than just historical argument, consisting in both fact and experience.

We found the objection that the whole issue is just a matter of personal interpretation unreasonable and self-refuting.

The charge that the transmission of the New Testament is similar to the kids' game *Telephone* is entirely false because, far from being what is usually seen as the "chain-link" form of transmission, the Gospel was given from the first to a community of people and transmitted as a community. The memory of the larger body (particularly that of the ancient Jews) has proven itself to be vastly superior to the memory of any single individual.

The objection that there is no reliable evidence for Jesus outside the New Testament rests upon a great misunderstanding of what the New Testament is and why it was formed. If there had been any other documents that were reliable, firsthand accounts of Jesus, they would have ended up in the collection in the first place. The New Testament is, by definition, the collected body of the most accurate and reliable sources available.

Moreover, we saw that this objection is inherently false and based purely upon historical ignorance. The sources outside the New Testament aren't numerous or in great detail, but they do exist. The surprise is not that there is so little evidence found outside the New Testament, but that there is so much, for the first group of believers wasn't yet a significant enough force to warrant any serious concern on the part of the pagan world.

We observed that the "other gospels" are not really

Gospels at all and are based upon historically inferior and very late sources.

Mentioned briefly were the "dying and rising savior gods" of the ancient world which the early Christians supposedly borrowed from when creating their own savior, Jesus. It is clear that these stories were just that – stories. Not only were they myths, entirely disconnected from real history, but the documents which preserve the fables are late, post-Christian productions. It's not successful to argue that they formed the basis for a single claim about Jesus.

We dismissed the false notion that since Bible scholars are already believers in Jesus, they can't be trusted. No generalizations can be made about those who study the Bible professionally. They represent a typical cross section of society in general.

We considered the so-called "other ways" to God and found that among the practices of the world's religions any evil can be condoned – even revered – so long as it stays camouflaged behind the façade of some religion somewhere. The distinction between good and evil fades from view entirely when all religions come to be regarded as equally true or right.

In addition, we discovered that no "common core" of values or truths exists among the smorgasbord of religious options. The notion that all religions are just variations of the same thing is merely part of popular folklore. We concluded that the "many ways to God" are, in reality, the many ways to the many gods. Only polytheism could result from this way of thinking. If there are many ways, then there are many gods. And if there are many gods, then the one true God does not exist. We have to choose the One or the many.

We found that faith in Jesus is unique among the other faith systems. It's based on real history, not prehistorical myth, legend, or religious fiction, but it's not limited strictly to historical investigation and historical answers. Genuine faith is a matter of personal experience and is open to validation in real life. If Jesus is alive and always present with his church as the Gospels claim he is, then he is objectively there for us to reach and to establish a relationship with. Even though God cannot necessarily be proved by one person to another, He reserves the right to prove Himself to each individual in a host of unique, tailor-made ways.

We dealt with the most common questions raised by thinking people and tried to show that a good question usually receives a good answer. Not every objection or question we can think of is dealt with directly by the New Testament. However, there are enough hints within the documents themselves to allow us to approach these questions and to assume that, even though we don't have precise answers to every one, God is always loving, fair, and just. His mercy and desire to save and forgive go far beyond our expectations and even exceed most of our recommendations.

Once we have exhausted our list of challenges and objections to the claims of Jesus, we are faced with the challenges God places before us: Are we really the truth seekers we claim to be? Do we love the truth wherever it may be found? Are we committed to following the evidence wherever it leads us? If the history of scientific discovery has taught us anything, it's this: Truth rarely follows the well-trodden path. Rather, it often appears in the crags and valleys or mountain peaks which are difficult to access. Sometimes it is only the bold and independent thinker, courageous enough to venture off the main road, who finds it.

By now, some of the following conclusions may have been reached:

Jesus' claims are so profound and so extravagant that there are only a few conclusions to be drawn. We cannot, for example, imagine that Jesus was just another unusual man in the first century who ended up with a few legends attached to his name. His claims are so astonishing, so high, so deep, so wide, and so unique that they surround no other figure in recorded history. Not only does the evidence work against such a theory, it would be impossible to account for the rise of such extraordinary claims about him had he not given some solid reason for their existence.

Since the claims of Jesus arose in the very heart of Judaism, it would have been entirely unexpected for someone to assert either for himself or for someone else that he was the unique, preexistent Son of God, co-Creator of the universe, and the very embodiment of God. Jesus' claims of authority were clear enough and strong enough to get himself crucified for blasphemy. His claims were a shock to everyone.

Unlike the Old Testament prophets who said, "Thus says the Lord," Jesus began his pronouncements with, "You've heard it said, but I tell you..." Jesus spoke like God Himself and referred to a unique relationship with the Creator unshared by other humans. No skeptic's theory of the "development of Christology" ever put forward does justice to the New Testament evidence as it is.

If we read the plain text just as it appears to us, we are confronted with a Jesus who was sent into the world in a supernatural way. He was born of a virgin, declared by God to be His beloved Son, and knew very early in life that he was in a special, unparalleled position with God the Creator. He was filled with the Spirit of God for special service, performed miracles unlike those of any previous prophet, was crucified, and died. But his physical body was raised from the tomb and he proved himself alive to his disciples as well as his skeptics. He ascended to the Father and reigns with Him until the end of the world when he will return and judge humanity prior to a recreation of the earth.

Every attempt to rework the material to make it more

palatable to modern tastes inevitably ends up transforming the claims into something far less than the earliest evidence suggests. We are in a position of either accepting the claims as they are, or tossing them all out in one piece. Picking and choosing which we can and cannot accept results in an exercise of total personal subjectivity. We can't create our own Jesus just because we don't like the one portrayed in the New Testament.

It's far more honest to reject the whole picture than to pretend that we can reconstruct Jesus the way we prefer him. If that's our inclination, then let's do what humanity has been doing from the beginning – simply create our own homemade religions, each to his own, adding what we like and eliminating what we don't. Let's continue the work of god-making as we've done since ancient times. Let's be our own prophets, our own gods, and our own interpreters of what is real and unreal. This is far superior to trying to rewrite the New Testament to make it say what we think it ought to have said.

Jesus is either the person who is clearly portrayed or he is not. If he's not, then let's dismiss him from our minds and get on with the business of constructing our own worlds. We may try with all our might to create our own realities, but as the old theologians of many centuries ago remind us (having tried their best for years to create their own), we can't tear up nature by its roots. In other words, what is real will always be real, and no amount of intellectual engineering can provide us an exit from God's created order.

If Jesus is who he said he is, let's begin to bring our thinking and our lives into line with what has been revealed. Let's adjust and adapt to the truth as it is. According to the teaching of Jesus, this is the only way to life. He is the way, the truth, and the life. No one comes to the Father except through him. No one comes to a knowledge of God the Creator unless Jesus the Son first grants permission for that to happen. To accept Jesus the Son is to accept God the Father, and to reject Jesus is to reject God. This is the foundation of all that we can call "Christian." There is no other form in which Jesus can be taken.

This is the principal scandal of the Christian faith, but it's also the source of its enormous power and basis of its great hope. It lays out unambiguously the facts we seek about God and declares that salvation and everlasting life with God are a gift freely offered by the Father through the Son. He says to us, "I've done it all for you; just reach out and take it!" He adopts us as His children and appoints us citizens of heaven. Anyone on earth who longs for it and receives it with the humility of a child is, in the end, given infinitely more than what they sought or even hoped for.

Ultimately, the great scandal of Jesus lies not so much in the realm of the intellect and its objections, but in the moral dimension. It's not the intellectual barriers which keep us from Jesus, the Son of God, but those which lie at the very core of our lives. Jesus is, in almost every way possible, an offense to our human pride and self-sufficiency. His word is so offensive to many not because it is unreasonable or without substance, but because it is so unwelcome. He takes salvation out of our hands and puts it firmly in his own. He beckons us to come to him with the readiness of a child, to receive a gift without payment, moral bartering, or personal merit.

No other faith or belief system on the planet offers anything remotely like this. Is Jesus the only way to God and salvation? Such a spectacular claim is our one and only hope.

appendix a

The Claims

The following is a more complete (although not exhaustive) list of the claims made by and about Jesus.

Romans

1:16–17	The Gospel is the power of God for the salvation of everyone who believes, both for the Jew and for the Gentile.
5:1–2	Access to God is gained through Jesus Christ.
8:18–25	His work of rescue extends to the whole created physical order.
16:26	The Gospel of Jesus is for all nations.

1 Corinthians

15:1–5	Paul received from others the historical facts of Jesus' death for sin, burial, resurrection from the dead, and appearances to the disciples.
15:3–8	The resurrected Jesus appeared to hundreds whose testimony could still be consulted.

2 Corinthians

5:19   In Christ, God was acting to reconcile the
            world to Himself.

Galatians

2:16   No human being will be saved by obedience to
            religious rites, rituals, or rules. Only trust in
            what Jesus did for us will lead us to God.

3:26   Humans become children of God only through
            faith in Jesus.

Ephesians

1:20–21   God raised Jesus from the dead and seated
            him at his right hand in the heavenly realms,
            far above all rule and authority, power and
            dominion, and every title that can be given,
            not only in the present age but also in the one
            to come.

2:13   Through Christ's sacrifice we are brought near
            to God.

3:11   God accomplished His eternal purpose in
            Jesus Christ.

4:10   Jesus Christ ascended higher than all the heav-
            ens in order to fill the whole universe.

Philippians

2:6–7   Jesus Christ, being in very nature God, conde-
            scended to take upon himself the form of a
            servant, being made in human likeness.

Colossians

1:15–17   He was the expressed image of the invisible
            God, head over all creation. All things were

created by him and for him. In him, all things in creation hold together.

1:19–20   God was pleased to have all His fullness dwell in him and through him to reconcile all things to Himself whether on earth or in heaven.

2:9–10   The fullness of the Deity dwelt in bodily form in him, the head over every power and authority.

4:13–18   He will come to earth again at the end of history.

2 Thessalonians

1:8–9   There will be eternal destruction for those who do no obey the Gospel of Jesus.

2:9–12   All those who refuse to love the truth about him will perish forever.

1 Timothy

1:15   Christ came into the world to save sinners.

2:3–6   There is only one God and only one mediator between God and man, Christ Jesus.

2 Timothy

1:10   He has destroyed death and brought life and immortality to light.

We now turn to a sampling of the evidence from the four Gospels.

Matthew

1:23   Jesus is called *Emmanuel*, God with us.

3:18   God calls Jesus His Son.

4:23   He healed every disease and sickness of the people.

Matthew

7:21	He called God "my Father."
10:1	He gave his disciples authority to drive out evil spirits.
10:32	Acknowledging or denying Jesus will be the basis for our being acknowledged or disowned before God.
11:27	All things are committed to Jesus by God. No one knows the Son except the Father, and no one knows the Father except the Son and those to whom Jesus chooses to reveal Him.
13:40	At the end of the age, the Son will send out his angels in judgment.
16:16	Jesus is the Christ, the Messiah, who has authority to give the keys of the kingdom of heaven.
17:1–13	God commands people to listen to Jesus, His Son.
19:28	At the end of history, his followers will help judge the world.
20:28	His life is given in death as a ransom for many.
23:24	He predicted Jerusalem's destruction (fulfilled in AD 70).
24:30–31	He will come again at the end of the world.
26:24	He was written about in the Old Testament.
26:53–54	He could have called on legions of angels to protect him from death.
26:63–64	He will sit on the right hand of God and come on the clouds of heaven.
28:18–20	All authority in heaven and on earth has been given to him. He commands his followers to make disciples of all nations, baptizing them in the name of the Father, the Son, and the Holy Spirit, teaching them his commands. He will be with them until the end of the Age.

Mark

1:7–9	He will baptize with the Holy Spirit.
1:11	He is God's Son.
2:5	He forgives sins.
3:11	Demons call him "the Son of God."
4:35–41	He controls the weather and natural phenomena.
6:30–44	He supernaturally feeds more than 5,000 people.
6:45–52	He defies gravity.
7:24–30	He determines whether or not a demon is cast out.
8:31–32	He predicts all the details of his death and resurrection.
8:35	He promises true life to any who will offer him their life.
9:36–37	Whoever welcomes Jesus, welcomes God.
13:31	His words will never pass away.
14:9	His Gospel will be preached throughout the entire world.
14:24	His death is offered in behalf of others.
14:36	He calls God his "Daddy" or "Papa."

Luke

1:33	His kingdom is eternal.
1:34–35	He is supernaturally born.
2:11	He is the Savior, Christ the Lord.
2:32	He is the light for the Gentiles and the source of salvation for all people.
2:49	As a boy, he was aware of an unparalleled relationship with God the Father.
3:17	The final judgment of humanity will occur with his return.

Luke

6:23	He promises that those rejected in this life for his sake will have great reward in heaven.
8:49–56	He has power over life and death.
9:1–2	He imparts God's power to others to cure diseases and drive out demons.
9:35	God's voice validates him and his words.
10:16	To reject him is to reject God.
10:22	No one comes to a knowledge of God unless Jesus grants permission.
23:42–43	He has authority to grant entrance into paradise.
24:5–7	His physical body is raised from death.
24:44	He was written about in the writings of Moses, the prophets, and the Psalms.
24:50–53	He ascended into heaven after the resurrection.

John

1:1	He is the Word who was with God in the beginning and who was God.
1:3	All that was made in creation was made through him.
1:14	The eternal Word, who was God, became human in Jesus.
1:14	He is the only Son from the Father.
1:29	He is the Lamb of God who takes away the sin of the world.
2:1–11	He manipulates and reorganizes molecules.
3:13	He came to earth from heaven.
3:16	He is God's only Son. Whoever believes in him will not perish, but will have eternal life.
3:17	God sent him into the world to save the world.

3:18	Salvation comes from believing in him, and eternal condemnation comes from not believing in him.
3:35	The Father loves the Son and has placed everything in his hands. Whoever rejects Jesus will not see life.
4:25–26	He is the Messiah.
4:42	He is the Savior of the world.
5:21	He gives life to whomever he chooses.
5:23	Whoever fails to honor the Son fails to honor the Father.
6:29	The principal work of God is for us to believe in Jesus, His Son.
6:38	He came down from heaven to do the will of the Father.
6:46	No one has ever seen the Father except the Son.
6:50–51	He is the bread from heaven who brings eternal life.
8:12	He is the light of the world.
8:50	He existed even before Abraham was born.
9:38	He is the object of human worship.
10:9	He is the gateway to salvation.
10:30	He and the Father are one.
12:44	To believe in him is to believe in God.
12:45	When we look at him, we see God.
14:6	He is the way, the truth, and the life. No one comes to the Father except through him.
16:15	All that belongs to the Father is his.
17:5	He enjoyed glory with the Father even before the creation of the world.
20:28	He was called "Lord" and "God."

In Luke's second work, traditionally called *The Acts of the Apostles*, he continues to record the work of the risen Jesus Christ in the life of the early church.

Acts

3:6	Physical healing is in the name of Jesus.
3:15	He is called "the Author of life."
3:21	He remains in heaven until his return to earth to restore all things.
4:12	Human salvation is found in no other name on earth than Jesus Christ.
17:30–31	Whereas prior to Jesus, God overlooked human ignorance about Himself, He now commands all people everywhere to repent and turn toward Him. All the world eventually will be judged on the basis of His Son.
28:28	Through Jesus, God sent salvation to all the nations.

The remainder of the New Testament echoes many of the same themes as the letters of Paul, the Gospels, and Acts:

Hebrews

1:2	He was appointed heir of all things, and through him God made the universe.
1:3	He is the radiance of God's glory and the exact representation of His being, sustaining all things by his powerful word.
1:4	He is superior to angels.
4:14	He is a great high priest who has gone through the heavens.
4:15	He was without sin.
5:9	He became the source of eternal salvation for all those who obey him.

9:26	He did away with sin by the sacrifice of himself.
9:28	He will appear again to bring salvation to those who are waiting for him.

1 Peter

3:19–20	He went and preached to the spirits in prison who disobeyed in the days of Noah.
3:22	He is now in heaven at God's right hand – with angels, authorities, and powers in submission to him.

1 John

2:2	He is the solution to the sin problem of the whole world.
2:23	No one who denies Jesus the Son has God the Father. He who confesses the Son has the Father also.
4:14	The Father sent His Son as the Savior of the world.
5:12	He who does not have the Son, does not have life.

Revelation

1:5	He is the ruler of earthly kings.
1:18	He holds the keys to death and Hades.
22:13	He is the Alpha and Omega, the beginning and the end (the same title claimed by the Lord God in 1:8).

appendix b

The Repentance of Rudolf Bultmann

What the name of Charles Darwin is to the field of biological science, the name of Rudolf Bultmann is to the world of New Testament study. Virtually every student of theology worldwide is introduced to the writings of German scholar Rudolf Karl Bultmann (1884–1976) and his students. He is considered by many the Grand Master of New Testament skepticism. In Germany he was hailed by many intellectuals as "the greatest event since Luther."

Bultmann is credited with launching the world-famous program of interpreting the "Jesus myths" for modern society by "demythologizing" the primary documents of the Christian faith. He stood like a colossus over academic biblical studies for much of the twentieth century. With variations, Bultmann's program was enthusiastically carried forward by his students who imagined themselves to be forging ahead with ever-increasing clarity on the ways legends and myths about Jesus entered the Christian tradition. His ideas form the underpinning of many who make pronouncements in the media asserting whether a particular story or saying of Jesus is authentic or not.

The movement of radical criticism has taken several different directions since his era, but he is the inspiration behind many of today's most vocal critics of the Bible. Building upon the literary principles of Bultmann, they assume that the vast majority of the recorded sayings and deeds of Jesus, although well-intentioned stories, are in the final analysis merely elaborate inventions of the early church. So extreme were Bultmann's methods and treatment of biblical texts that he was criticized even by his old schoolmate, philosopher Karl Jaspers.

But did this giant of doubt have a change of mind and repudiate his entire teaching career before he died in 1976? Three lines of converging evidence may be considered:

(1) Reports in Germany of such a change;

(2) Bultmann's apparent predisposition to return to a traditional faith; and

(3) the remarkable events occurring at his funeral.

Stories have been circulating in and around Germany to the effect that in his closing days Bultmann "converted," turned entirely against his life's work, and even sent a final message to some of his closest students apologizing for all that he had ever taught about the New Testament.

The reports first came to my attention in the spring of 2004 while living in Basel, Switzerland. A theology student and friend of mine, Dietrich Wichmann, heard the account of the change of mind from one of Bultmann's former students and teaching assistants (now an octogenarian) who was passing through Basel. We were immediately intrigued and began to pursue the matter.

Dietrich set out to cover the contacts associated with

Tübingen, Germany (to where this particular version of the story could be traced), while I interviewed people in Marburg (where Bultmann spent most of his teaching career). Eventually, we ended up speaking to people in other German cities such as Herleshausen, Göttingen, and Münster. Further connections led us even to people now living in New York.

Here is what we found. The original information we received was apparently a somewhat corrupted version of an account that could be tracked back to a hospital in Tübingen (Tropenklinik Paul-Lechler-Krankenhaus). There, Professor Ernst Käsemann, one of Bultmann's principal students, had been receiving care for a heart condition just prior to his death in February 1998. A nurse working closely with Professor Käsemann heard unequivocal statements from a visiting German clergyman that Bultmann had "converted" or "repented" some time before he died. A second and apparently independent report (also traceable to Tübingen) claimed that he had made a private apology to a few of his students following his change. The exact identity of the clergyman and what his relationship to Bultmann or Käsemann was could not be established.

As for famed biblical critic Käsemann himself, it appears from some of his final comments that much of his thinking was controlled by a lifetime of intense suffering. At the age of nine, he was plunged into deep loneliness by the loss of his father in World War I. His oldest son Dietrich was snatched from him at age nine by diphtheria. Later, his thirty-year-old daughter Elisabeth was tortured and brutally murdered in Argentina for political reasons. One cannot help but speculate as to what extent such acute personal trauma influenced his very public theological skepticism.

It is not known whether Käsemann ever heard the account of Bultmann's "repentance." We know only that in the end there was animosity between the two men, most likely precluding Käsemann as a personal confidant of his former mentor.

We were unable to find anyone in Marburg still alive who was a close acquaintance of Bultmann in the very last days of his life either to verify or to dispute the story of his repentance. Over the 28 years since his death at age 92, most of the clues had grown cold. Many of his pastors, students, and closest friends had passed on, and those associates who knew him best during his career had little or no access to him in his final years. His personal reader admitted to having had no contact in the last three years of Bultmann's life and his current biographer in the last four to six years. Even some of his immediate family members had very little close association until the very end.

When some who knew him personally were told the story of his alleged end-of-life turnabout, they responded in a variety of ways, ranging from, "That's only mythology," (an interesting choice of words) to, "It seems improbable," to, "Yes, it could have happened." Apparently, it would not have been out of character for Bultmann to change his mind on important theological matters without ever clearly saying so. Even during the peak of his influence, other theologians of his day suggested that he did exactly that (Hordern, 23).

But did he change his mind here? Is this a true story or merely an unfounded rumor split into two separate traditions? If true, was the secret taken to the grave with the last of his closest students? There would have been very strong reasons for those left behind not to reveal the change, since entire careers and international reputations based upon his teaching hung in the balance. To this day, he and his students are still revered as icons in the German academic world.

The trail of evidence for these two versions of the story ended with the nurse and the unnamed clergyman. But the more we continued our probe along other lines into

Bultmann's alleged "repentance," the more evidence came to light, all seemingly pointing in the same direction. Month by month, scattered bits and pieces of the puzzle were assembled to form a more coherent picture of the great scholar's mysterious last days. Since other potentially valuable sources of information were not able to be consulted (some were unwilling to speak to us), it is entirely possible that more information could surface in days to come.

We learned that during his career Bultmann spoke wistfully to a few of his closest students about the loss of the faith of his youth. This was never an insignificant matter to him and apparently played upon his mind his entire professional life. He came from a family of staunch believers (his paternal grandfather was a missionary to Africa and his maternal grandfather was a pastor in the pietistic tradition). As a young, devout Lutheran, he was severely affected by the shocks of World War I as well as the corrosive influences of skeptical German theologians Johannes Weiss, Wilhelm Heitmüller, Wilhelm Hermann, and Adolf von Harnack. He was relatively late in publishing any significant works since, unlike his father, he was slow to accept much of the German liberalism of his day. It seems that he never fully reconciled with much of it and always remained a potential defector from the camp.

Some of the many people who visited Bultmann at his home on Calvinstrasse 16 during his closing days observed that the man who was so vocal and adamant about his views during his professional life had slipped into an ever-deepening and reflective silence, while in full possession of his mental faculties to the very end. What was he thinking during those long days as blindness was closing in upon him and the glories of this world were literally fading from view? Was he pondering the bitter accusations made against him during his lifetime that, much against his original intent, he had helped to destroy the church in Germany and served to undermine the faith of countless numbers of people worldwide? Like the wandering prodigal in the parable of Jesus, had he returned home to the simpler faith of his youth after retracing his steps leading away from the biblical Jesus to radical skepticism? He had three years after his wife's death to do little more than grieve, remember, and think. What took place in his heart of hearts during those literally thousands of hours of solitary introspection or reevaluation as death was approaching?

What appear to have been his most eloquent final statements about Jesus, the New Testament, and his personal faith come from the remarkable events which occurred at his funeral.

On Wednesday, August 4, 1976, at the Matthäuskirche in Marburg, only a few instrumental pieces, his favorite hymn, a motet by Bach, and readings of Scripture were heard. Dr. Christian Zippert was presiding. Bultmann, who spent his entire career arguing vigorously (some would say pugnaciously) that the New Testament could not possibly be understood correctly without a great deal of academic explanation (particularly his own), ordered that the texts be read without comment. Contrary to the very heart of his earlier theology, there was to be no demythologizing, no preaching, and no interpretation. This one fact stood out as extraordinary in the minds of virtually all those interviewed. One theologian present at the funeral admitted to being puzzled by this omission since, in his words, "Bultmann's theology demanded it."

After Bultmann parted from this life, the Scriptures read to the congregation were left to speak for themselves. Whatever he thought about the biblical texts and their need for radical reconstruction and demythologizing during his long teaching career, he wanted them just as they were to have the last word. Printed on the lead page of the worship bulletin was the first in a series of surprises, the request by Bultmann himself that "this hour should belong entirely to the Word of Holy Scripture" (Dorhs, 88).

The order of worship (Dorhs, 86) was as follows:

> Prelude: J. S. Bach's organ choral, *Vor deinem Thron*
> Choir Piece: Four-part motet by Melchior Franck,
>   *Herr, nun lässest du...*
> Pastor's Greeting
> Scripture Readings (interspersed with pieces by Mozart and Bach):
> 2 Corinthians 4:6–11
> 2 Corinthians 5:1–7
> John 5:21–25
> Bach motet: *Jesu, meine Freude* (sung by Bultmann's family)
> Silent Prayer
> Unison Reading of Psalm 103
> Hymn: Georg Neumark's *Wer nur den lieben Gott lässt walten* (verses 1–4, 7)
> Scripture Reading: 1 Corinthians 7:29–31
> Postlude: Organ piece by J. S. Bach

The choice of texts to be read forms what looks like a theological last will and testament. Since his eyesight was nearly gone, the actual selection process was carried out by his daughters, but he knew the readings and endorsed them. He approved each passage, then emphasized that they be read and left to stand on their own. He was particularly concerned that there be absolutely no praise of him or his life's work. He left this directive with Pastor Zippert. Perhaps this accounts for Bultmann's partiality for the arresting phrase "life of vain endeavor" that he knew well from his beloved motet by Bach. Why would he want these words included in his funeral with a complete absence of any biographical or vocational references?

For many years it had been Bultmann's practice to use the life of the deceased as the basis for important lessons imparted to those still living. This deliberate elimination of a biographical account, a stated connection between the dead and the living as a relationship between teacher and student, was a complete departure from his own custom when performing funerals. The earthly life of each person was key for him. However, he clearly forbade for his own service what he consistently had required for those of others (Dorhs, 88).

As for the Scriptures and their arrangement, they create the distinct impression of a sermon outline:

> 2 Corinthians 4:6–11
> 2 Corinthians 5:1–7
> John 5:21–25
> 1 Corinthians 7:29–31

The sanctuary was filled with Bultmann's colleagues, intellectuals from around Europe, dignitaries, friends, and family. The summary testament (sermon?) Bultmann wanted them all to hear was as follows:

> For God, who said, "Let light shine out of darkness," made his light shine in our hearts to give us the light of the knowledge of the glory of God in the face of Christ. But we have this treasure in jars of clay to show that this all-surpassing power is from God and not from us. We always carry around in our body the death of Jesus, so that the life of Jesus may also be revealed in our body. For we who are alive are always being given over to death for Jesus' sake, so that his life may be revealed in our mortal body.
>
> 2 Corinthians 4:6–11

Now we know that if the earthly tent we live in is destroyed, we have a building from God, an eternal house in heaven, not built by human hands. Meanwhile we groan, longing to be clothed with our heavenly dwelling, because when we are clothed, we will not be found naked. For while we are in this tent, we groan and are burdened, because we do not wish to be unclothed but to be clothed with our heavenly dwelling, so that what is mortal may be swallowed up by life. Now it is God who has made us for this very purpose and has given us the Spirit as a deposit, guaranteeing what is to come. Therefore we are always confident and know that as long as we are at home in the body we are away from the Lord. We live by faith, not by sight.

2 Corinthians 5:1–7

For just as the Father raises the dead and gives them life, even so the Son gives life to whom he is pleased to give it. Moreover, the Father judges no one, but has entrusted all judgment to the Son, that all may honor the Son just as they honor the Father. He who does not honor the Son does not honor the Father, who sent him. I tell you the truth, whoever hears my word and believes him who sent me has eternal life and will not be condemned; he has crossed over from death to life. I tell you the truth, a time is coming and has now come when the dead will hear the voice of the Son of God and those who hear will live.

John 5:21–25

What I mean, brothers, is that the time is short.... For this world in its present form is passing away.

1 Corinthians 7:29–31

That Bultmann would allow these readings (particularly those on resurrection) to stand on their own is astonishing in light of how he treated such texts at the height of his career. Yet it was customary, at least in later years, for him to allow all resurrection texts to stand alone when used in funerals (Dorhs, 88). It is illuminating to examine how he interpreted each of these passages in his earlier theological writings.

If the unexpounded Scripture readings were a disturbance to the hearers, how much more was the music. Bultmann requested what in the end had become his favorite hymn, Georg Neumark's *Wer nur den lieben Gott lässt walten* ("If Thou But Suffer God to Guide Thee"). It was introduced with strong emphasis as the hymn that had come to mean so much to him. The text in English by Catherine Winkworth reads as follows:

Verse 1
If thou but suffer God to guide thee
And hope in Him through all thy ways,
He'll give thee strength, whate'er betide thee,
And bear thee through the evil days.
Who trust in God's unchanging love
Builds on the rock that naught can move.

Verse 2
What can these anxious cares avail thee,
These never-ceasing moans and sighs?
What can it help if thou bewail thee
O'er each dark moment as it flies?
Our cross and trials do but press
The heavier for our bitterness.

Verse 3
Be patient and await His leisure
In cheerful hope, with heart content
To take whatever thy Father's pleasure
And His discerning love hath sent,
Nor doubt our inmost wants are known
To Him who chose us for His own.

Verse 4
God knows full well when times of gladness
Shall be the needful thing for thee.
When He has tried thy soul with sadness
And from all guile has found thee free,
He comes to thee all unaware
And makes thee own His loving care.

Verse 7
Sing, pray, and keep His ways unswerving,
Perform thy duties faithfully,
And trust His Word: though undeserving,
Thou yet shalt find it true for thee.
God never yet forsook in need
The soul that trusted Him indeed.

In view of Bultmann's great fondness for the hymns of Gerhard Tersteegen or Paul Gerhardt, it was a further wonder to some present that nothing from their works was selected. Their mystic theology or poetry was not anywhere evident (Dorhs, 87).

Although Bultmann specified no preaching or eulogy, he allowed the Scriptures, the hymn, and Johann Sebastian Bach to do a great deal of speaking. A competent musician in his own right, he would have the family gather in the mornings as he played a piece from Bach on the piano or harpsichord. After a lifelong passion for the music of Bach, he had become a master of every word and nuance of his motets.

The musically literate congregation was given weighty commentary from Bultmann's most beloved motet, *Jesu, meine Freude* ("Jesus, My Joy"), clearly suggesting a type of highly personalized faith testimony. With words rather than instruments being supremely important, motets were classic vehicles for delivering heavy loads of theology and Christian witness. Every word was to be articulated with crystal clarity and with the utmost dramatic effect. This motet stands out as a choral sermon on death and resurrection, powerfully interpreting the Apostle Paul's theology in Romans 8. It highlights the insignificance of death, the coming resurrection of the physical body, and the believer's everlasting communion with Jesus his Lord.

With vivid word painting and unparalleled musical architecture evident throughout the work, Bultmann chose in this piece one of the most eloquent and explicit songs of repentance in the entire library of sacred music. Coming from deep within the soul of Bultmann, the famed doubter and demythologizer of Jesus, the words were more than startling. As the service progressed, few were prepared for what was to follow:

> Therefore, there is now no condemnation for those who are in Christ Jesus, in order that the righteous requirements of the law might be fully met in us, who do not live according to the sinful nature but according to the Spirit.
>
> Romans 8:1

> *Verse 1*
> Jesus, my salvation,
> And my heart's possession,
> Jesu, all my joy,
> With what great desiring,
> With what deep despairing,
> I have longed for thee!
> Lamb of God, o wellbelov'd,
> Here on earth no joy allures me;
> Nothing less can please me.

> There can be no ungodliness in those who truly are in Jesus Christ, those who follow not their passions, but the Spirit.
>
> Romans 8:4

Verse 2
Lord, thou dost defend me
From the storms around me
And the enemy.
Let the devil taunt me;
Let the world affront me;
Jesus is with me.
Though storms crash, though lightnings flash,
And though sin and hell afflict me,
Jesus will protect me.

Because through Christ Jesus the law of the Spirit of life set
me free from the law of sin and death.

Romans 8:2

Verse 3
Yes, though Satan hates me,
Yes, though death awaits me,
Yes, though I may fear!
Rage then, world, with cursing!
I stand here rejoicing,
For my help is sure.
For God's power holds me secure;
Earth and hellfire must keep silence,
Though they raged with violence.

You, however, are controlled not by the sinful nature but by
the Spirit, if the Spirit of God lives in you. And if anyone does
not have the Spirit of Christ, he does not belong to Christ.

Romans 8:9

Verse 4
Go from me, all treasure!
Thou art all my pleasure,
Jesu, my desire.
Go, all vain pretenses!
You offend my senses,

And I will not hear.
Sorrow, pain, cross, death, and scorn,
Though here they may overcome me,
Shall not take thee from me.

But if Christ is in you, your body is dead because of sin, yet
your spirit is alive because of righteousness.

Romans 8:10

Verse 5
So good night, affections,
All the world's attractions,
For you give no joy.
And good night, transgression,
Sins of my commission,
Come no more to me.
So good night, all pride and might.
And, o life of vain endeavor,
Now good night forever.

And if the Spirit of him who raised Jesus from the dead is
living in you, he who raised Christ from the dead will also
give life to your mortal bodies through his Spirit, who lives
in you.

Romans 8:11

Verse 6
Leave me now, o sadness,
For the Lord of gladness,
Jesus, comes to me.
Those who love the Master
Find all their disaster
Turned to hope and joy.
Though I earn abuse and scorn
Thou must also suffer passion,
Jesu, my salvation (*Bach*, 16–20).

Surely, Bultmann could not have been oblivious to the impact such an extraordinary service would have upon the illustrious gathering at the Matthäuskirche. The entire event appeared carefully conceived, constructed, and executed, and his aim must have been achieved. According to Pastor Zippert, the congregation left the church that day utterly "stunned."

At the graveside, there was a brief reading (again without interpretation) taken from the Gospel of John 11:25–27:

> "I am the resurrection and the life. He who believes in me will live, even though he dies; and whoever lives and believes in me will never die. Do you believe this?"
>
> "Yes, Lord," she told him, "I believe that you are the Christ, the Son of God, who was to come into the world."

It is clear from family members that Bultmann felt that some personal, spiritual preparation was necessary for death and that he believed himself completely ready for his own passing and an open-armed reception into the presence of God. In a personal letter (dated March 9, 1991) his daughter Heilke Bultmann stated that he had met death "internally prepared and composed." She added:

> He said our life here was bound to earthly time. No one here could conceive eternity, but one could confidently feel secure in God and hope to be lifted up into "God's time" after earthly life. This is approximately how he expressed himself to me and this is how he died with confidence (Dorhs, 86).

He was laid to rest high on a hill in the huge, forested Ockershausen cemetery, a few blocks from his home on Calvinstrasse. Bultmann appears to have taken his final cue from the parting sentiments of his mother-in-law, whose grave lies next to his and his wife's. What took a collection of Scriptures, a hymn, and an extended motet to say to his survivors and friends, she expressed in one simple thought: The Lord saves the best wine for last (John 2:10).

The same passage Bultmann had chosen three years earlier for his wife Helene's funeral, contrasting the temporal, passing kingdom with the everlasting one yet to come, was repeated in his obituary in Marburg's newspaper, the *Oberhessische Presse*, for Monday, August 2, 1976:

> So we fix our eyes not on what is seen, but on what is unseen.
> For what is seen is temporary, but what is unseen is eternal.
> 2 Corinthians 4:18

There are several nagging questions which still hang over this entire story: If Bultmann did experience such a profound transformation, then why didn't he just spell it out clearly? Why would everyone be kept guessing? Can there be any plausible explanation for such an indirect route? There are several possibilities:

• He was known for not clearly announcing his changes of thought to the world. He was even criticized by other scholars for this personal idiosyncrasy.

• As a very private person by nature, he never felt obliged to explain himself to others. Born and raised in Oldenburg/Lower Saxony, he represented well his area's customs, known over Germany as exhibiting an exaggerated, often obsessive protection of personal privacy. Even today, visitors to the region are struck by this characteristic of its inhabitants.

If asked directly whether he had experienced some sort of personal repentance and returned to a traditional faith in Jesus, he most likely would have said, "That's my business!" – if he even bothered to respond to the question. For traditional

Oldenburgers, such public disclosures of highly private matters were simply out of the question.

• From a wider view, such a general announcement of a very personal repentance, fairly ordinary in some other cultures, was not commonly made on the level of German intellectual society where he spent his professional life. It was unsuccessful when tried. In a celebrated case in Marburg, roughly around the time of Bultmann's death, a reputable New Testament scholar who had recently come to faith in the traditional Jesus of the New Testament stood up and publicly renounced the entire school of Bultmannian higher criticism. This confession was utterly incomprehensible to other scholars and resulted only in confusion. It was as if reason itself had been repudiated. The event was immediately disregarded by the theological community and thereafter written off as too absurd to take seriously.

Bultmann's chosen course of action seems the most intelligent and effective way of communicating his final testimony of faith. He must have known that any other strategy would have resulted in a general dismissal of his mental faculties, forbearance of his age, failure of will in the face of death, or the like. He had a great many hours to play out in his mind this one last chess game and to determine the most powerful presentation of his closing profession of the faith he had spent a lifetime trying to understand.

appendix c

The Bishop's Move: The Case of John A. T. Robinson

If there was a counterpart to Rudolf Bultmann in the English-speaking world it would be John A. T. "Honest to God" Robinson (1919–1983), so nicknamed for his book of that title published in 1963. It sent shock waves through the Christian community because it was written by a popular and scholarly Bishop of the Anglican Church and dean of Trinity College, Cambridge. In it he openly disputed much of what churchgoers everywhere recognized as the Gospel of Jesus and credited Bultmann for paving the way for others to follow. For his efforts he was as widely acclaimed by skeptics and theological liberals as he was condemned by believers.

The admiration between Robinson and Bultmann appeared to be mutual. In a personal letter written to Swiss theologian Karl Barth, Bultmann expressed satisfaction that his ideas had been taken up by Robinson and introduced into the current theological debate about God (Jaspert, ed., 1994, 310).

Based upon his radical views of the 1960s, Robinson is still cited as the inspiration and authority behind many of today's most outspoken critics of historic Christian faith.

What is not usually mentioned is that as his career advanced and his knowledge of New Testament history grew, his opinions on some key issues seemed to drift increasingly toward a more traditional view. His book on the early dating of the New Testament documents (Robinson, 1976) was not favorably received by many of his first admirers, and his work on the essential historical trustworthiness of the New Testament, published the following year, is treated now as though it never existed. Most younger students of theology are completely unaware that the latter book was even written. His book *Where Three Ways Meet* records what he thought and preached as late as six weeks before he died of cancer (Robinson, 1987).

There is a long history of prominent thinkers who in their earlier years expressed the most skeptical views on the Bible, but grew beyond their doubts either in their closing years of life or in the prime of their scholarly labors. The more they learned and the broader their range of experience, the more of the Gospel they believed. Honest and consistent questioners eventually get around to doubting their own doubts.

It must be admitted, too, that great skeptics, doubters, and even hard-boiled atheists are just as human as anyone else. When in the end each of us is forced to look directly into the cold-blooded stare of death, unexpected and dramatic transformations of mind or heart can occur rapidly as our perspective on everything changes. Our final days of life can be as formative as our first months and years of childhood. Gazing for the first time from the brink into the great black abyss focuses our minds and clears away the irrelevant as nothing else can.

The academic world tends to have the memory of an elephant regarding the earlier stages of development of the world's most eminent skeptics but is often utterly forgetful of the latter. This short-term memory loss would not be tolerated for an instant – it would in fact be regarded as the height of scholarly irresponsibility – if it occurred in any field of study other than theology.

notes

1: The Human Factor

1. Letter to William Graham, Down, July 3rd, 1881. Cited in *The Life and Letters of Charles Darwin Including an Autobiographical Chapter*, Francis Darwin, ed., vol. 1 (New York: D. Appleton and Company, 1887), 255. See Alvin Plantinga's essay "Darwin, Mind and Meaning," *Veritas Forum, UCSB*, http://www.veritas-ucsb.org/library/plantinga/Dennett.html (accessed December 2005).

2. G. B. Caird, "Biblical Language and Imagery," (lecture series, Mansfield College, Oxford University, Oxford, 1973–74).

2: Getting the Questions Right

1. W. S. Duvekot, "Heeft Jezus zichself voor de Messias gehouden?" (Amsterdam: Assen, Van Gorcum, Prakke & Prakke, 1972).

2. W. F. Albright, quoted in an interview with *Christianity Today*, January 18, 1963, 3.

3. F. F. Bruce, *The New Testament Documents: Are They Reliable?* (Grand Rapids: Eerdmans, 1968); Josh McDowell, *The New Evidence That Demands a Verdict* (Nashville: Thomas Nelson Publishers, 1999); John Warwick Montgomery, *History and Christianity* (Downer's Grove: InterVarsity Press, 1965); Lee Strobel, *The Case for Christ* (Grand Rapids: Zondervan, 1998).

4. Bruce, *The New Testament Documents*, 16–18; Josh McDowell, *A Ready Defense* (Nashville: Here's Life, 1993), 45.

5. For more examples of intervals between original writings and dates of earliest significant texts, see F. W. Hall, "MS Authorities for the Text of the Chief Classical Writers," in *A Companion to Classical Texts* (Oxford: Clarendon Press, 1913), 199 ff.

6. Frederic Kenyon, *Handbook to the Textual Criticism of the New Testament*, 2nd ed. (London: Macmillan & Co., 1912), 5.

7. Quoted in Montgomery, *History and Christianity*, 26–28.

8. J. Harold Greenlee, *Introduction to the New Testament Textual Criticism* (Grand Rapids: Eerdmans, 1964), 54.

9. W. M. Ramsay, *St. Paul the Traveler and the Roman Citizen* (Grand Rapids: Baker Book House, 1951), 7–8.

10. Millar Burrows, *What Mean These Stones?* (New York: Meridian Books, 1956), 176.

11. Nelson Glueck, *Rivers in the Desert* (New York: Farrar, Strauss & Cudahy, 1959), 31.

12. Quoted in Bruce, *The New Testament Documents*, 91–92.

13. Quoted in Montgomery, *History and Christianity*, 32.

14. A. N. Sherwin-White, *Roman Society and Roman Law in the New Testament* (Oxford University Press, 1963), 189.

15. Caird, "Biblical Language and Imagery," (lecture series).

16. H. N. Ridderbos, *The Speeches of Peter in the Acts of the Apostles* (London: Tyndale Press, 1962).

17. See Bibliography for competent historical defenses of the resurrection: J. N. D. Anderson, Stephen Davis, Gary Habermas and Anthony Flew, G. E. Ladd, Lee Strobel, Frank Morrison, Josh McDowell.

18. Pinchas Lapide, *The Resurrection of Jesus: A Jewish Perspective* (Wipf & Stock Publishers, 2002).

19. Stephen T. Davis, Daniel Kendall, and Gerald O'Collins, *The Resurrection: An Interdisciplinary Symposium on the Resurrection of Jesus* (New York: Oxford University Press, 1997), 207.

3: Objections

1. Bernard Ramm, "Can I Trust My Old Testament?" *The King's Business*, February 1949, 230–231.

2. W. F. Albright, *Archaeology and the Religion of Israel* (Baltimore: Johns Hopkins University Press, 1956), 176.

3. W. F. Albright, *The Archaeology of Palestine* (Baltimore: Penguin Books, 1960), 229.

4. Bruce, *The New Testament Documents*, 114.

5. Cited from Robert J. Miller, ed., *The Complete Gospels: Annotated Scholars Version* (Polebridge Press, 1994).

6. See Ronald Nash, *The Gospel and the Greeks* (Richardson, TX: Probe Books, 1992), originally published in 1984 under the title *Christianity and the Hellenistic World*; J. Gresham Machen, *The Origin of Paul's Religion* (New York: Macmillan, 1925); Bruce M. Metzger, *Historical and Literary Studies: Pagan, Jewish, and Christian* (Grand Rapids: Eerdmans, 1968).

4: What's the Alternative?

1. A. Ashforth, *Witchcraft, Violence, and Democracy in South Africa* (Chicago: University of Chicago Press, 2005), 202–206, 220.

2. By the phrase "law of the jungle" I intend what most people today understand by it – that which evolutionary theory has construed it to mean. It implies the brutality and competition which pits one creature against another, where in the end only the strongest survives. But when it was first coined by Rudyard Kipling in his *Jungle Book* series, he meant something positive by it – the law and order by which wild creatures instinctively act. The two very different meanings illustrate the problem dealt with here.

   Kipling was portraying a world created by the one God who stamped certain patterns of orderly behavior upon His creation. Modern evolutionary theory usually assumes a world without the superintendence of this one orderly God. With a few exceptions, it imagines either no God at all or a variety of deities of our own making, each to his own, with no one god better or worse than any other. Clearly, to abandon belief in this one true God in favor of whatever god (religion) one chooses is to end up in a "jungle" of conflicting deities (and conflicting moralities) with only the stronger overpowering the weaker.

3. Huston Smith, *The Religions of Man* (New York: Harper & Row Publishers, 1965), 353.

4. I've discussed this in my book *Reincarnation vs. Resurrection* (Chicago: Moody Press, 1984).

5: Common Questions

1. See Kenneth Scott Latourette's massive work, *A History of the Expansion of Christianity*, 7 vols. (Harper & Brothers Publishers, 1937–45).

2. George Barna, *Grow Your Church from the Outside In* (Ventura: Regal Books, 2002), 43.

bibliography

Albright, W. F. *Archaeology and the Religion of Israel.* Baltimore: Johns Hopkins University Press, 1956.

Albright, W. F. *The Archaeology of Palestine.* Baltimore: Penguin Books, 1960.

Albright, W. F. *Christianity Today* (January 18, 1963).

Anderson, J. N. D. *The Evidence for the Resurrection.* Downers Grove: InterVarsity Press, 1966.

Bach, Johann Sebastian. *Motets*, translated by Jean Lunn, Margaret Schubert, and Roger Clement. Neuhausen/Stuttgart: Hänssler-Verlag, 1999.

Barna, George. *Grow Your Church from the Outside In.* Ventura: Regal Books, 2002.

Blomberg, Craig. *The Historical Reliability of the Gospels.* Downers Grove: InterVarsity Press, 1987.

Bruce, F. F. *The New Testament Documents: Are They Reliable?* Grand Rapids: Eerdmans, 1968.

Bruce, F. F. *Jesus and Christian Origins outside the New Testament.* Grand Rapids: Eerdmans, 1974.

Burrows, Millar. *What Mean These Stones.* New York: Meridian Books, 1956.

Caird, G. B. "Biblical Language and Imagery." Lecture series, Mansfield College, Oxford University, Oxford, 1973–74.

Clifford, Ross. *The Case for the Empty Tomb*. Claremont: Albatross, 1991.

Davis, Stephen T., Daniel Kendall, and Gerald O'Collins. *The Incarnation: An Interdisciplinary Symposium on the Incarnation of the Son of God*. New York: Oxford University Press, 2002.

Davis, Stephen T., Daniel Kendall, and Gerald O'Collins. *The Resurrection: An Interdisciplinary Symposium on the Resurrection of Jesus*. New York: Oxford University Press, 1997.

Dorhs, Michael. "Über den Tod hinaus: Grundzüge einer Individualeschatologie in der Theologie Rudolf Bultmanns." Ph.D. diss., Marburg University. Frankfurt am Main: Peter Lang GmbH, 1999.

Geisler, Norman and Thomas Howe. *When Critics Ask*. Wheaton: Victor, 1992.

Glueck, Nelson. *Rivers in the Desert*. New York: Farrar, Strauss & Cudahy, 1959.

Green, Michael. *"But Don't All Religions Lead to God?"* Grand Rapids: Baker Books, 2002

Green, Michael. *Christ Is Risen: So What?* Kent, England: Sovereign World, 1995.

Greenlee, J. Harold. *Introduction to the New Testament Textual Criticism*. Grand Rapids: Eerdmans, 1964.

Habermas, Gary and Anthony Flew. *Did Jesus Rise from the Dead? The Resurrection Debate*. San Francisco: Harper & Row, 1987.

Hall, F. W. "MS Authorities for the Text of the Chief Classical Writers." In *A Companion to Classical Texts*. Oxford: Clarendon Press, 1913.

Hordern, William. *New Directions in Theology Today*. Vol. 1. Philadelphia: The Westminster Press, 1966.

Jaspert, Bernd. *Karl Barth – Rudolf Bultmann Briefwechsel 1911–1966*. Theologischer Verlag Zürich, 1994.

Kenyon, Frederic. *Handbook to the Textual Criticism of the New Testament.* 2nd ed. London: Macmillan & Co., 1912.

Kenyon, Frederic. *The Bible and Archaeology.* New York: Harper, 1940.

Ladd, G. E. *I Believe in the Resurrection of Jesus.* Grand Rapids: Eerdmans, 1975.

Lapide, Pinchas. *The Resurrection of Jesus: A Jewish Perspective.* Wipf & Stock Publishers, 2002.

Latourette, Kenneth Scott. *A History of the Expansion of Christianity.* 7 vols. Harper and Brothers Publishers, 1937–45.

Machen, J. Gresham. *The Origin of Paul's Religion.* New York: Macmillan, 1925.

McDowell, Josh. *A Ready Defense.* San Bernardino: Here's Life, 1993.

McDowell, Josh. *The New Evidence That Demands a Verdict.* Nashville: Thomas Nelson Publishers, 1999.

Metzger, Bruce M. *Historical and Literary Studies: Pagan, Jewish, and Christian.* Grand Rapids: Eerdmans, 1968.

Miller, Robert J., ed. *The Complete Gospels: Annotated Scholars Version.* Polebridge Press, 1994.

Montgomery, John Warwick. *History and Christianity.* Downer's Grove: InterVarsity Press, 1965.

Morrison, Frank. *Who Moved the Stone?* Grand Rapids: Zondervan, 1987.

Nash, Ronald. *The Gospel and the Greeks.* Richardson: Probe Books, 1992.

Ramm, Bernard. "Can I Trust My Old Testament?" *The King's Business,* 1949.

Ramsay, W. M. *St. Paul the Traveler and the Roman Citizen.* Grand Rapids: Baker Book House, 1951.

Ridderbos, H. N. *The Speeches of Peter in the Acts of the Apostles.* London: Tyndale Press, 1962.

Robinson, John A. T. *Honest to God.* SCM Press and Westminster Press, 1963.

Robinson, John A. T. *Redating the New Testament.* Philadelphia: Westminster Press, 1976.

Robinson, John A. T. *Can We Trust the New Testament?* Grand Rapids: Wm. B. Eerdmans Publishing Company, 1977.

Robinson, John A. T. *Where Three Ways Meet.* Nashville: Abingdon Press, 1987.

Sherwin-White, A. N. *Roman Society and Roman Law in the New Testament.* Oxford University Press, 1963.

Smith, Huston. *The Religions of Man.* New York: Harper & Row Publishers, 1965.

Snyder, John. *Reincarnation vs. Resurrection.* Chicago: Moody Press, 1984.

Strobel, Lee. *The Case for Christ.* Grand Rapids: Zondervan, 1998.

index

about the author

Pastor, author, and conference speaker John Snyder has spent the last thirty years in preaching, teaching, discussion, and debate over the Jesus question. He has taught New Testament studies at New College, Berkeley, and has also pastored and planted churches in California, New York, and Switzerland.

Dr. Snyder earned his Master of Theology and Master of Divinity degrees from Princeton Theological Seminary, and received his Doctor of Theology degree from the University of Basel, Switzerland. He has contributed articles to academic journals and newspapers including *Theology Today*, *Dialog*, *Theologische Zeitschrift*, *Journal of the Evangelical Theological Society*, *The Washington Times*, and others.

Dr. Snyder is the author of *Reincarnation vs. Resurrection* and *These Sheep Bite*, as well as the forthcoming *Resenting God* and *Storm Rider: Surviving and Thriving After Life's Catastrophes*.

He is a happily married husband and father of two children. His wife and daughters are also published authors. Dr. Snyder and his family share their time between California, New York, and Europe.

Printed in the United States
78431LV00002B/253-348